Prai

THE WANDERDAYS

JOURNEY TO FANTOME ISLAND

"Storytelling at its finest – a heart pounding, edge-of-your-seat adventure with an important eco message at its heart."
Laura Noakes, author of *Cosima Unfortunate Steals a Star*

"A dynamic and daring tale powered by friendship and sibling strength. I couldn't put it down!"
Richard Pickard, author of *The Peculiar Tale of the Tentacle Boy*

"Fantastic! A modern classic in the making."
Cat Gray, author of *Spellstoppers*

"Filled with fantastical creatures, brilliantly brave kids and dastardly villains."
Jo Clarke, author of *Libby and the Parisian Puzzle*

"An absolute delight."
Melissa Cristina Márquez, author, marine biologist and "Mother of Sharks"

For my three mizuko, who joined me
as I wrote this book. You're forever
a part of my own story.

First published in the UK in 2024 by Usborne Publishing Limited, Usborne House, 83-85 Saffron Hill, London EC1N 8RT, England. usborne.com

Usborne Verlag, Usborne Publishing Limited., Prüfeninger Str. 20, 93049 Regensburg, Deutschland VK Nr. 17560

A CIP catalogue record for this book is available from the British Library.

ISBN 9781803708089 JFM MJJASOND/24 8775/1

Printed and bound using 100% renewable energy at CPI Group (UK) Ltd, Croydon, CR0 4YY

FSC www.fsc.org MIX Paper | Supporting responsible forestry FSC® C171272

THE WANDERDAYS

JOURNEY TO FANTOME ISLAND

CLARE POVEY

USBORNE

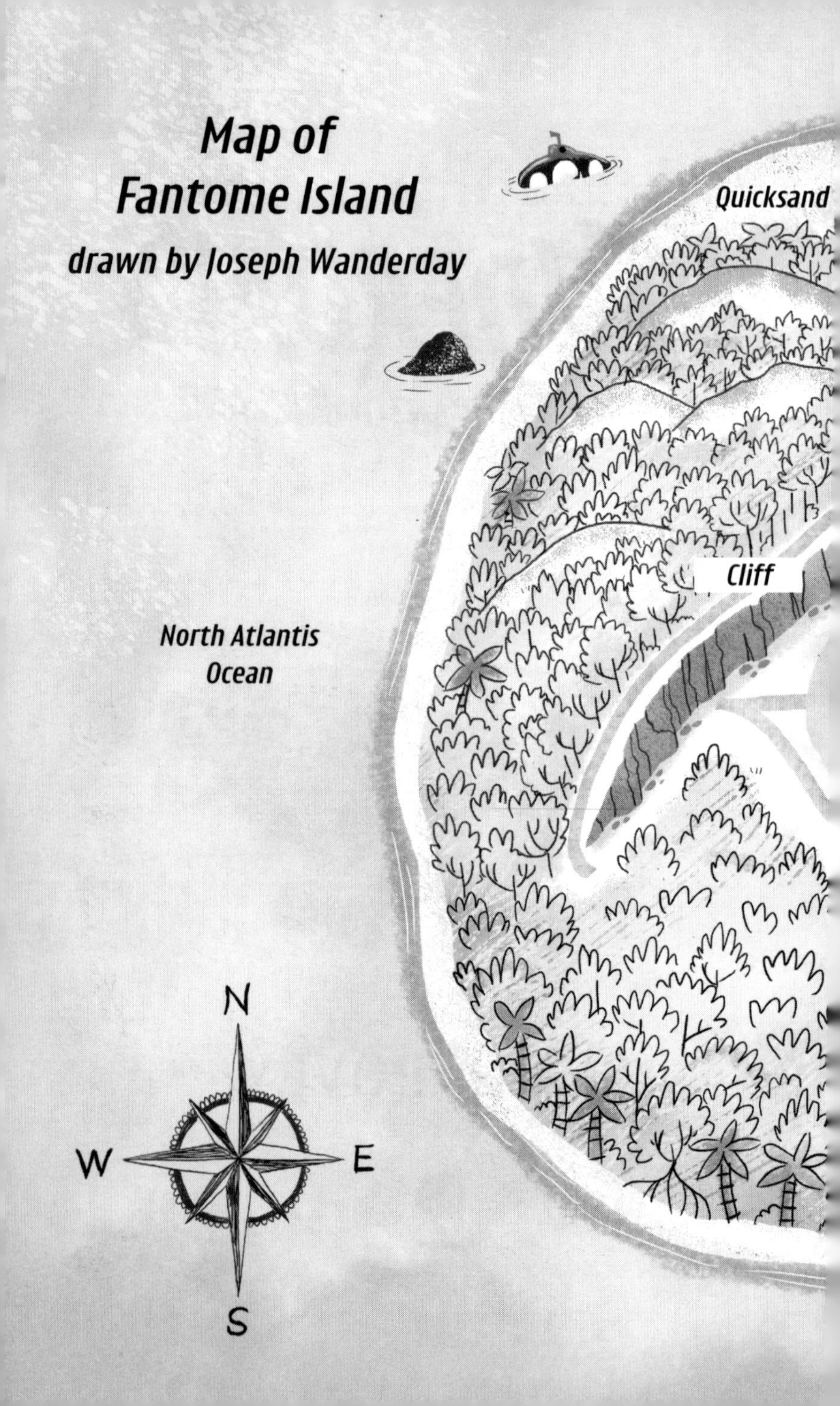
Map of
Fantome Island
drawn by Joseph Wanderday
Quicksand
Cliff
North Atlantis
Ocean
N
W
E
S

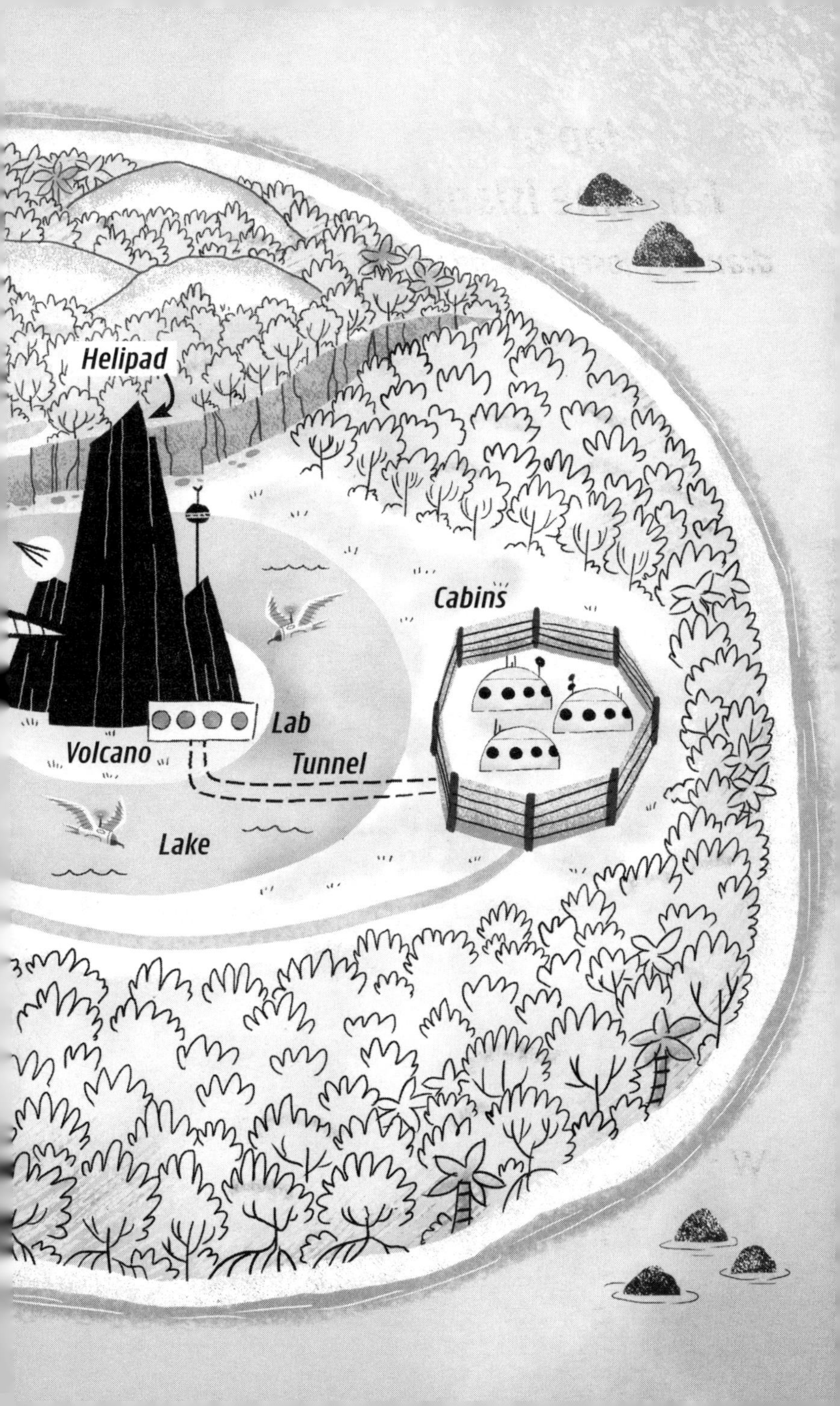
Helipad
Cabins
Lab
Volcano
Tunnel
Lake

"When the last tree is cut, the last fish is caught, and the last river is polluted; when to breathe the air is sickening, you will realize, too late, that wealth is not in bank accounts and that you can't eat money."

Alanis Obomsawin

Chapter 1

BAD NEWS BEFORE BREAKFAST

Bad news was forbidden in the Wanderday household until after breakfast. That was the main rule that Flo and Joseph Wanderday had been brought up to respect. Pancake stacks and veggie sausage sandwiches filled you up first, so your well-fed stomach only had room for a little bit of the badness.

But this morning, a warm July day in the port city of Brinemouth, Flo had only just poured the pancake batter into the pan when a terrible feeling crept over her. She checked the starfish-shaped kitchen clock and panicked. It was half past seven. When Mum was away on expeditions, she called every other morning at precisely quarter past seven. Never early, never late;

the famous Nellie Wanderday was always on time. She'd never missed a morning call, not even when The Titans, the famous eco-expedition team that she'd once been a part of, had been stuck in a snowstorm at the top of Mount Ante. But the phone hadn't yet rung and Flo couldn't help but wonder why. It had now been two days since she'd last spoken to Mum and worry tried to take hold of Flo.

Mum's latest expedition was about deep-sea ecosystems in the North Atlantis Ocean and she'd gone with her crew aboard *The Ariel*, her trusty green research boat. Maybe a dive was taking longer than expected? Or she'd discovered something exciting and lost track of time? Mum was like that, putting the ocean before herself; exploring and trying to protect it at all costs.

A loud knock on the door pulled Flo's mind back to shore. It did no good to think in maybes when her brother worried enough for both of them. Mum would call soon and explain everything.

"Jojo!" Flo poked her head out of the kitchen and down the long, blue hallway that connected every room in the apartment. "Can you get that? I'm making *our* breakfast!" Her little brother could sleep through an apocalypse. If zombies ever invaded the Fortunia, the yellow limestone apartment building where they lived, they'd probably mistake Joseph for one of their own.

Flo flipped the pancake, her frustration simmering as she heard no movement from her brother's bedroom. She loved Joseph more than most twelve-year-olds probably loved their ten-year-old siblings, and was always there when he needed to talk through his unwanted thoughts. Nevertheless, she'd put a lump of rotting seaweed under his mattress if she burned breakfast because of him.

The door creaked under a flurry of knocks and Flo admitted defeat. If they got any louder she'd miss the sound of the phone if Mum called. *When* she called.

"I'm coming!" Flo hurried down the hallway, her trusty camera swinging from the blue strap round her neck. She carried it everywhere she went and, at night, she even tucked it under her spare pillow. Only her best friend Funmi knew that.

Flo had secretly been thrilled when Mum had announced her expedition at the same time Dad had received an invitation to exhibit his paintings at a gallery out of the city. Her parents' trips only overlapped by two days, but she'd fantasized about those forty-eight hours of freedom. Unfortunately, Flo had forgotten about her extended family, the residents of the Fortunia, and each hour since her parents' departure someone had knocked with home-cooked meals or offers of homework help. If she had to eat another one of Mrs Hearst's lasagnes, she'd stick a carrot in her own eye.

But today was the last day, well half-day, of school before the summer holidays arrived. Flo and Funmi had made so many plans – rooftop sleepovers, samphire foraging in the salt marsh, riding the new big drop at the Aderemi Adventure Park (owned by Funmi's parents) – and Flo was going to capture every moment on film. This was the summer she'd make her first ever documentary and become the next Wanderday film-maker. Just like Mum.

"Open this door before I knock it down!"

Funmi's voice startled Flo. They usually met in the lobby before school and Funmi was always late, sleeping through her alarm. Why was she here early, shouting and knocking on the door like a demon?

"Hold your seahorses!" Flo fiddled with the key in the lock. Her fingers grew clammy and she kicked the bottom of the door until it finally opened.

Funmi flew in to the apartment. She was usually as light as the candyfloss they ate on the pier, but her dark-brown eyes were narrow and she anxiously twisted the ends of her long box braids as she paced. Her red painted nails were bitten down to the quick.

"What's going on?" Flo asked.

"Have you watched this morning's news?"

The strange look on Funmi's face startled Flo. "No. I'm waiting for Mum to call. Why?"

Funmi's mouth dropped open. "Your— I don't know how to say this." She grabbed Flo's hand and pulled her down the hallway.

"What's going on?" Flo's question was met with silence as they reached the movie room. It was her favourite place at home and she often spent evenings curled up under the glow-in-the-dark stars on their colourful beanbags (clownfish orange for Flo and sargassum brown for Joseph), in front of the floor-to-ceiling projector screen.

Now, the movie room felt cold and lonely as she flopped down on her beanbag. Funmi hadn't explained anything yet, but the uneasiness Flo was feeling started to make sense. Mum still hadn't called and now Funmi was here, anxious and unable to get her words out. Bad news was coming and Flo hadn't even had breakfast; her stomach was as empty as a washed-up seashell.

Funmi grabbed the remote and the screen lit up, bathing the windowless room in brightness. An image of Mum's boat appeared. The news reporter spoke in sullen, staccato sentences, but Flo couldn't hear anything over the loud rushing in her ears.

Then Funmi squeezed in next to her and Flo willed herself to focus. She took a breath, looked, properly, at the screen and clung on to each of the reporter's words.

"*Contact was lost with* The Ariel *research boat belonging to Nellie Wanderday, acclaimed ocean explorer and film-maker, approximately forty-eight hours ago in the North Atlantis Ocean. The boat was last spotted heading north when its automatic tracking system went offline. All attempts at contact since have failed. International police now consider* The Ariel *a missing vessel and a full investigation is underway.*

"*Nellie Wanderday arrived on our screens twenty years ago with her debut film* The Wanderday Chronicles, *which documented her travels around the world as a young oceanographer.*

"*After the film's release, Wanderday was recruited by philanthropist and former television presenter Sir Frederick Titan, to join his aptly named eco-expedition team The Titans. The team was created and led by Sir Frederick after he left his successful travel presenter career behind to pursue his true passion of helping countries combat climate change.*

"The Titans were a team of explorers, including marine biologists, scientists and environmental experts, known for their cutting-edge research and education projects across the globe. Their television show The Titans Tour, *which documented their travels and good planet deeds, ran for ten seasons.*

"But the reign of The Titans was cut short when prominent team member and scientist Percy Parish died in a sailing accident three years ago. A decision was made to disband and members of The Titans went their separate ways.

"Both Percy and Nellie, like Sir Frederick, were born and bred in Brinemouth and are considered local treasures.

"Since then Nellie Wanderday has travelled the world's oceans with her own crew. At the time of her boat's disappearance, she was researching deep-sea ecosystems in the North Atlantis Ocean. It is feared the boat may have been damaged, or destroyed, by the harsh climate of this area. Rogue waves and whirlpools have often destroyed boats here, leaving passengers lost at sea.

"We hope that Nellie's latest adventure has not come to a murky end."

Sadness and anger bubbled inside Flo. "This isn't

happening!" She grabbed the remote and threw it at the screen. "Mum's boat can't be missing! This has to be a mistake."

Yet her words didn't feel true. She'd felt off since Mum had missed their call. Flo had tried to push the feeling away, but she could no longer escape the facts. Mum hadn't called because she couldn't. All communication with *The Ariel* was lost. The boat was missing. Mum was missing.

"They'll find your mum and her crew." Funmi hugged Flo tight. "She'll be home in a few days. Just like she planned."

A thousand images floated around inside Flo's brain. As soon as one image of *The Ariel* being sucked into a whirlpool disappeared, another bubbled up. In the middle of the chaos, she pictured Mum: her long black hair always tied back to see through her camera lens; her walrus-like laugh that both embarrassed and delighted Flo and Joseph; and how she always smelled of the disgusting kelp gobstoppers she ate.

Flo allowed herself a minute and then, holding on to those precious images, she built a dam in her brain to block everything bad out. From this moment on, she needed to be stronger than ever before. She had to be her own life jacket to keep herself afloat in the oncoming storm.

Flo stood and wiped her eyes. From the hallway, the phone rang like a warning sign that had come too late. Any hope she'd had of hearing Mum's voice had all but trickled away.

"I better go and answer that." She nodded at Funmi to follow. "Then we have to wake Joseph and tell him."

Chapter 2

THE MANY LIVING NIGHTMARES OF JOSEPH WANDERDAY

Joseph woke up and, for a second, everything was fine. Sunshine streamed through the stained-glass window, reflecting a parrotfish on his bedroom wall. It was a sign of a good day.

Joseph looked for signs everywhere. Nothing bad happened when it was sunny and, if he clicked his fingers ten times before bed each night, everyone he loved would be safe. This morning, he held on to the good day for a second longer.

And then the stone sea wall around his mind crumbled away and the bad thoughts flooded in.

What if Isaac realizes he doesn't want to be my best friend?

What if Mum doesn't come back from her expedition?

What if I fail the marine biology exam?

Today's exam would determine whether he'd get into Dr Moray's summer school for young marine biologists next year. The thought of spending six weeks with his hero was more excitement than his brain could manage. Joseph had dreamed of it ever since Mum had taken him to an event with Dr Moray at the Brinemouth Amphitheatre for his eighth birthday.

While the intruding thoughts battled in his mind, Joseph crawled out of bed and turned on his speaker. Dr Moray's latest audiobook continued to play.

"*The deep ocean holds secrets so rare that they only reveal themselves to explorers with good intentions. There are precious materials scattered across the abyssal plains, creating ecosystems where unique creatures thrive. There are seamounts – underwater mountains that rise from the sea floor like the fist of a god. There are creatures with unique, unbelievable abilities that humans can only dream of.*

"*And the trenches, at the very bottom of the ocean floor, are the ultimate unknown. A place of darkness, where the living must find a way to survive. Here is uncharted territory, a place with no rules, that has driven grown adults to obsession, dreaming of a new world that is theirs to conquer.*"

Joseph searched for his school uniform in the piles of

dirty clothes littering his floor. His bedroom was as chaotic as his mind. Not for the first time, he wished to be more like Flo. Confidence flowed through her veins. She was a carbon copy of Mum, fearless and assured, and Joseph was…

Well, what was he exactly?

He found his uniform stuffed behind his desk and got changed. Last night's snack, a bag of chocolate seahorses from Cousteau's Confectionery, was smeared down his school shirt and he failed to scrub the smudge away. He only raided the kitchen cupboards when his mum was away on an expedition. Chocolate helped ease thoughts of *The Ariel* hitting the tip of an iceberg, or a wave pulling Mum and her crew down into the hadal zone, the deepest area of the ocean.

The jaunty tone of his alarm clock made Joseph jump. Dread rushed through him when he saw the time. He'd missed Mum's morning phone call! Now he wouldn't be able to talk to her for another two days.

Seeking comfort, Joseph turned to The Titans poster hanging next to his bed. It was taken from their trip to the island of Salin, which had been Mum's first expedition as a Titans team member. She'd quickly become the viewers' favourite after rescuing a family of otters from an oil spill. There wasn't a kid in Brinemouth who didn't have the same poster plastered on their bedroom walls, with The Titan's motto *Acta Non Verba* – Deeds Not Words in Latin – printed at the bottom, to remind them to look after the planet every day.

"I suppose this is the only way I can talk to you today." Joseph placed his hand against the image of his mum. "I miss you. Hope you're not discovering too many cool things without me."

In the poster Mum wore a bright green wetsuit and a giant grin. Sir Frederick Titan's thick white beard was full of sand and, kneeling at the front, was Percy Parish, his eyes shining like amber glass as he cradled a baby otter.

"And you too Uncle Percy." Mum's old teammate had understood Joseph in a way that most people couldn't. There'd been a hole in his heart ever since Uncle Percy had died. He'd gone too quickly and without warning. Joseph would've done anything to hear one of his uncle's cheesy motivational quotes again, especially ahead of today's exam.

"The biggest mountain you'll ever climb is in your own mind," had been one of their shared favourites. They'd both understood that climb more than most people.

Joseph could've stayed in his memories for ever, but a burning smell returned him to reality. "Flo!" He pulled on his trainers and grabbed his rucksack. "Breakfast is burning!" He flung open his bedroom door and almost crashed right into his sister.

"What are you—?" Joseph stopped when he saw Flo's puffy face.

"Jojo." Her voice was hoarse. "I need to tell you something."

Joseph noticed Funmi lingering behind Flo, her forehead creased with worry. Another bad sign.

When Flo's eyes finally met his, Joseph understood. She didn't have to say it; he could read his sister like his favourite marine biology book.

"Mum."

And that was the last thing Joseph Wanderday said before everything went blurry and the ground rose up to meet him like a razor clam.

Chapter 3

ANEMONES AND ANSWERS

Flo and Funmi placed Joseph on the sofa. The living room had long been overtaken by plants and flowers; heart-shaped green leaves crept across the walls, wrapping round frames, while wooden shelves creaked from stacks of photography books and pots of paint brushes.

Flo grabbed the glass plant mister and directed the nozzle at Joseph's face.

"Hey!" His eyes flitted open and he batted the droplets away. "What're you doing?"

"Bringing you back to life." She helped him sit up. "You feeling better?"

"You hit the ground pretty hard." Funmi shook out her hand. "We tried to catch you, but ended up with a couple of squashed fingers instead."

"Sorry," Joseph said, rubbing his head. His dark hair stuck up in tufts, reminding Flo of a Mary River turtle. They were endangered and grew algae on their heads like a little green mohawk. Mum had told her and Joseph about the turtles after returning from a research trip last winter.

Flo bit her lip. Everything reminded her of Mum. From Joseph's hair to the anemones that blossomed on the balcony. They were Mum's favourite flowers and she always took one away on expeditions, enclosing the petals in her golden locket. *So my home is always close to my heart.*

The longing Flo felt almost split her in half and she squeezed her brother's hand.

The smile on Joseph's face flickered. "What's happened to Mum?"

"The news report said that *The Ariel*'s tracking device is offline and no one's been able to contact them for over a day." Flo couldn't bring herself to say that the boat was missing. It felt too scary, too real.

Joseph whimpered.

"It's only on the TV because your mum's famous," Funmi said. "It wouldn't be a news story if it was a normal person."

Flo nodded. "Exactly. *The Ariel*'s tracking and communication systems should come back on soon and she'll call us."

Joseph shot up from the sofa and swayed on his feet. "What about Dad? Is he coming home? Oh tides! Why didn't anyone tell us sooner? Why did we have to find out from the news?"

"One thing at a time." Flo grabbed his arm and gently pulled him back to sitting. "Dad called a few minutes ago right after I saw the news. The police contacted him late last night, but he didn't want to wake us. He said *The Ariel* is an old boat and the systems have crashed before, but they always come back on. He's catching the next train. He'll be home tomorrow morning."

Joseph said nothing, apart from his stomach growling in response.

"Shall I go get us some grub?" Funmi asked. "There's some unburned pancakes left. I know you lot take breakfast seriously around here."

"Thanks." Flo smiled gratefully. Even if she and Funmi hadn't grown up in the Fortunia together, Flo knew they would've found each other and become best friends another way.

"I told Mum not to go to that far north in the

Atlantis," Joseph said. "What if the Devil's Diamond got her?"

"The legends of the Devil's Diamond aren't real." Flo kept her voice measured. "The ocean doesn't make people disappear. There aren't any monsters lurking underwater. How can someone who loves science believe such crazy stories?"

Joseph gritted his teeth. "I *know* it's not rational, but the deep is a world of its own. Anything could be down there."

"Jojo! That's not helping."

But Joseph didn't stop. "What if the *The Ariel* sank? Mum and the rest of her crew could be seriously hurt."

"Enough!" Flo shouted.

The door creaked open and Funmi placed a plate of pancakes on the coffee table. "I'm going to go check on my sis. Baba and Mum left for work early, so if I don't wake her she'll sleep until this evening. You two okay?"

"We'll be fine," Flo replied. "Meet you downstairs in a bit?"

"You bet." Funmi slipped out of the living room.

As Joseph nibbled the edge of a pancake, Flo walked over to the balcony door. It was another day in Brinemouth; the city was busy with the hum of electric cars and the whining noise of the funicular that transported citizens down to the waterfront. Flo looked to the west and saw the scaly, iridescent dome of the Wanderday Institute, the oceanography and film-making centre that Mum had opened two years ago, poking out between the treetops of Plankton Park.

How did it feel like an ordinary day when the earth had turned upside down? Flo had told Joseph that they'd hear from Mum soon, but she didn't know if that was true. It was out of her control. Everything was.

"I try so hard to not always think the worst," Joseph whispered, his voice breaking apart like the rotting flotsam that washed up in the industrial port. "But it's hard. The bad thoughts get stuck and get louder."

Flo sat back down next to him and hugged him tight. "You never have to apologize. I'm sorry for shouting. Your thoughts aren't who you are. It's just all those mixed-up chemicals in there." Flo tapped his forehead. "Whatever you need to say, you say it, alright?"

Joseph wiped his nose with his sleeve. "So what are we going to do now?"

It was an impossible question. No one had written a manual on what to do when your mum's boat goes missing in the ocean. But the look in Joseph's eyes forced Flo to think smarter. She couldn't let him worry more and she definitely didn't want him to see her own concerns.

"We get ready and go to school," Flo declared. She stood and tied her ash-blonde hair into a ponytail. Wisps of stray hair, cut too short during one of her spontaneous self-haircuts, fell forward. "You've got your exam. Mum wouldn't want you to miss it."

"Shouldn't we stay home in case the police come?"

"Dad said they're calling him with updates and they won't come here until he gets home." Flo pulled her brother to his feet. "But I was thinking we should do some investigating of our own when we get back from school. Maybe there's more information in Mum's studio about this expedition. She didn't tell us much, did she? We know what ocean she was exploring, but maybe we can find something, a map or coordinates, that shows *The Ariel*'s exact route. It might help narrow the search."

Joseph's face brightened and Flo knew that he was remembering the detective games they used to play with Mum and Dad. They'd collect clues around the Fortunia and present their evidence to Mum, who always played the judge with a little too much enthusiasm.

Flo was glad to see a smile back on her brother's face. Investigating would be a good distraction for him. For both of them.

As Joseph wolfed down the pancakes, Flo opened the balcony door. Heat hit her in the face as she plucked a blue anemone petal and slipped it into her pocket. Like Mum, she wanted to keep home close to her heart. Home was everything. It was every nook and cranny of the Fortunia, from the creaking elevators to the rubbish chutes.

When everything was off-kilter, home was an anchor. Flo couldn't let herself drift.

"Let's go."

With her arm round Joseph, they headed off to face the day.

Chapter 4

LOOSE LIPS SINK SHIPS

The elevator dinged, announcing its arrival at the Fortunia's ground floor. The doors jutted open and Flo hurried to the lobby. Joseph jogged beside her, and Funmi, who'd met them in the elevator on the way down, trailed behind as she fixed the broken strap of her watch.

The lobby was completely empty. It was normally busy with residents rushing around and delivery people traipsing in and out of the post room. Why wasn't Dame Judi Varda, the Fortunia's elegant, ancient heiress, walking her five dogs? And where were Mr and Mr Povowski? They always ate their breakfast bagels in the courtyard.

"It's a ghost town." The silence unsettled Flo, as though the day had realized that something was wrong and scraped away all its usual routine.

"Weird," Funmi said. "Even Pilcher isn't here."

Flo walked over to Mr Pilcher's concierge cubbyhole. A piece of paper was stuck to the top of his desk.

"*Resident meeting on the roof terrace to discuss the Wanderday problem*," Flo read. "*Normal concierge service will resume at 8.30 a.m.*"

Joseph scrunched up his nose. "The Wanderday problem? What's that about?"

"Everyone's probably just arguing over who'll babysit us until Dad gets home." Flo tutted. "We're hardly a *problem*."

A muffled cough echoed from the other side of the lobby. Flo tensed and Joseph scuttled across the floor like a surprised crab. Funmi grabbed an umbrella from the concierge cubbyhole.

"Who's there?" Cautiously, Flo led them towards the source of the noise. Funmi was by her side with the umbrella raised like a sword. No reply came. There was a scuffling from behind the potted palm trees in the lobby corner. Flo readied herself and pushed back the leaves.

Hiding behind the plants was Isaac Kessler, Joseph's best friend. He was crouched on the floor, his black curls hiding half his face.

"This is," Flo searched for the right word, "unexpected."

Joseph snorted. "Mate, what *are* you doing? You scared us."

Isaac dropped his magnifying glass as he sprang up. "I thought I saw a twenty-two-spot ladybird. Honestly, that's it. I'm not doing anything weird."

"We weren't thinking weird until you said it," Funmi replied, eyeing Isaac like a bad smell.

As though he'd snapped out of a haze, Isaac gasped and reached for Flo's hand. "Gosh, Flo. Joe. I heard about your mum's boat going missing. I'm so sorry. I was on my way to yours—"

Flo recoiled. She didn't need, or want, to hear the word sorry.

Isaac ran his hands through his hair. "Anyway, my dad said you should use the worker's entrance round the back. You'll avoid all of *them* that way."

Flo arched an eyebrow. "Who's them?"

"The journalists." Isaac led the way through the plants towards a small square window. Isaac's dad was the Fortunia's building manager and knew its every nook and cranny. Dealing with the demanding residents took up most of Mr Kessler's time – Flo had seen him being harassed by Dame Varda only last week about installing a doggy-friendly escalator in her apartment – so Isaac didn't see his dad much at home.

Flo stood on her tiptoes and pushed the window open further to find a shoal of paparazzi and journalists in the courtyard.

"I was here first," the woman at the front in a bright salmon two-piece suit shouted. "*The Daily Mouthful* broke the news first. I should interview the Wanderdays."

Flo recognized the walking salmon as Char Lamprey, the co-host for *The Daily Mouthful* news show. She'd heard Mum say, on several occasions, how Char sucked up gossip in Brinemouth like a Hoover.

"News doesn't work like that!"

Flo followed the other voice to a tall woman at the back of the crowd. Most of her face was hidden by a large green sun hat. "Plus, an exclusive source contacted me not twenty minutes ago."

"Oh yeah?" Char Lamprey pouted. "What did your source say?"

The woman pulled her hat even lower. Did she not

want to be recognized? "Nellie Wanderday's last radio transmission to the coastguard forty-eight hours ago confirmed the boat was on course for its anchor and that all nine of the crew were in good form."

"Nine?" Pressure squeezed against Flo's head like she'd just gone diving without a helmet. Had she heard the journalist correctly?

"Who's your source at the coastguard?" Char Lamprey demanded. "What else did they say?"

The woman ignored the question and batted away the other journalists as she moved stealthily through the crowd. Flo tried to follow her movements, but the woman was quick, too quick, and disappeared from view.

Flo closed the window and marched back through the palm trees, her mind swirling as she sat down in one of the lobby armchairs.

"What were they saying?" Joseph asked. "I couldn't hear anything."

Funmi perched on the armrest and placed her palm against Flo's cheek. "You look as green as algae. What's up?"

"A journalist said Mum's last radio to the coastguard counted nine people on *The Ariel*." Flo paused. "But there's always been eight crew members. Right?"

Joseph nodded. "Right."

Each one of Mum's team brought a unique skill.

Belle, with her organized brain, made the perfect expedition manager.

Sal kept everyone fed on trips with their delicious plant-based meals.

Twins Agnès and Clio were a formidable camera and sound technician duo.

Krystyna was the boat's best pilot.

Indira was a marine engineer. She cared for the boat like it was a living being.

Mona was a qualified doctor, healing everything from coral cuts to cases of the bends.

And Mum, oceanographer and film-maker, made eight.

"So there was an extra person on the boat before it went missing?" Joseph's fingers started to twitch. "What if this person turned off the tracking system on purpose? What if they wanted to make Mum vanish?"

"Hang on." Isaac held up his hands. "Don't jump to conclusions! Maybe your mum made a mistake when she counted?"

"Mum doesn't make mistakes," Flo said. "She knows her crew inside out."

"Everyone makes mistakes." Funmi patted her shoulder. "Especially when they've been at sea for weeks."

The lobby clock chimed half-past eight and the sound brought Flo back to life. The journalists outside the Fortunia were hungry for a scoop, but she only wanted to speak to the woman in the green hat. Why had she mentioned Mum's last radio message to the coastguard and then disappeared again? Was it just a rumour or was the woman telling the truth? Flo's thoughts then turned to Mum. Could she have made a mistake counting her crew? Or had someone else, with bad intentions, come aboard *The Ariel*?

The question of who would want to make Mum's boat disappear was a thought that Flo didn't want to dwell on. She couldn't let her brain jump to conclusions; she needed to find out more.

Flo got to her feet. "I know it might feel impossible, but you need to get to school and ace that exam, Jojo." She held out her hands to him. "Do you want me to transfer your worries?"

When Flo had first realized that her little brother had more worries than most, she'd been determined to make him feel better. And so she'd devised a plan.

Any time that Joseph felt overwhelmed by thoughts, Flo would simply take his hands and squeeze all of the bad thoughts out of him and into her. The worry transfer, she'd called it.

Joseph smiled as Flo squeezed his palms tight. She shook his hands like there was an electric current running between the pair of them.

"All done. I'll hold on to your worries until you come back home."

"Thanks, sis."

"The next tram to Harbourview is in five minutes." Isaac nervously glanced at the clock above Mr Pilcher's cubbyhole. If we miss it, we'll miss the exam!"

"You coming?" Joseph asked Flo.

She shook her head. "I need to speak to that journalist and find out more about Mum's last message to the coastguard."

"Oh." The disappointment in his voice stung Flo. "But you said we'd investigate together."

"And we will! I promise." She crossed her fingers. "As soon as you get home from your exam. I'm just going to get us a head start."

"Fine." Joseph sighed. "Just be careful, okay?"

"Always."

"Joe!" Isaac was already running. "We've got to go!"

Flo felt relieved as she watched Joseph follow Isaac out of the lobby. The exam would help concentrate his mind on something other than what might've happened to Mum.

She turned back towards the Fortunia's front door and discovered that Funmi hadn't moved.

"Aren't you going too?"

Funmi craned her head in the direction of the journalists swarming closer. "As if I'm leaving you alone with all those vultures."

"You sure? I don't want you to get into trouble with your parents."

Funmi rolled her eyes dramatically. It made Flo think of a mantis shrimp and how the tiny marine animals were capable of rolling their eyes in every single direction. "This is way more important. Me missing one day of school before summer can't do that much damage to the Aderemi Adventure *brand*." She shrugged. "My parents are working night and day on the new Kraken Water Coaster and Ameyo doesn't care about anything other than whether Louis in 10B has messaged her back."

Flo laughed. "You double sure?"

"I'm always sure. Now don't question me again."

Flo smiled at her best friend, grateful that she'd never have to do anything in life alone.

Funmi clapped her hands. "Shall we invite this grubby lot in and find that journalist?"

Flo grabbed her Fortunia key card from her pocket. She pictured the outrage on Mr Pilcher's face when he returned to his cubbyhole, but she still swiped the card. She had to do this. The front door jutted open and Flo shielded her eyes just in time to see the crowd move towards her.

Somewhere amid this chaos was the woman with the green sun hat, the woman who knew all about Mum's last message before *The Ariel* disappeared.

That was certainly worth getting in trouble for.

Chapter 5

BITTER BULLIES AND THE DR MORAY QUESTION

Joseph hurried under the sculpted whalebone gates of Harbourview Academy. His shirt clung to his back with sweat after the sprint through the city's old town, and its winding cobbled streets, to get to school on time.

"Ready for this?" Isaac asked as they traipsed through the playground.

"Sort of." Getting into Dr Moray's marine biology summer school had been the most important thing in Joseph's life until this morning. Now he felt unanchored, but he tried to hold on to what Flo had said. Mum wanted him to ace this exam, so he would do exactly that and they'd all celebrate together when she came home.

There were a hundred eyes on Joseph as he walked up the steps to the main door. He tried to ignore the whispers, but each one was like a knife prising him open.

"Nemo's mum got eaten by the kraken."

"My parents said The Ariel*'s probably at the bottom of the ocean by now."*

"Maybe she's finally run away. I would if I had to look at Nemo's face every day."

Joseph's eyes tingled with tears. The nickname Nemo had stuck with him ever since Pierre Crowfly, the self-proclaimed coolest kid at Harbourview, had coined it five years ago. Their class had visited the National Science Museum and the teachers had forgotten that Joseph was in the toilet as they packed the other kids back onto the coach. He'd waited with security until Mum picked him up hours later. Ever since that day, Joseph had been Nemo. In Latin, nemo meant *nobody* and his stupid nickname was a constant reminder that he was entirely forgettable.

Suddenly Isaac was no longer by his side. He was standing on the top step, blocking the school door.

"If any of you have something to say," Isaac said, "please come and say it to *my* face."

Joseph looked at Isaac in shock. He'd never seen him speak up like this at school. The pair of them usually kept to themselves, staying below the radar and out of Pierre's way.

"If I hear any of you say one more stupid thing about my best mate's mum it won't be sea monsters you'll need to worry about. So keep your mouths shut."

The playground turned as silent as stone. The other kids shuffled along, heads down, before disappearing into the winding school corridors.

Joseph clapped Isaac on the back. "Thank you. But where did that come from?"

"Honestly?" Isaac shrugged. "I have no idea."

Joseph pushed open the door to the Frederick Titan Hall of Champions. The sports hall had been renamed after one of Frederick's generous donations to the school. Frederick had spread his wealth across the city; in fact the only building in Brinemouth that hadn't benefitted from a Frederick Titan donation was the Wanderday Institute. Mum had wanted to go it alone after The Titans had disbanded, to show Brinemouth and the rest of the world that she could stand on her own two feet. Joseph admired her for that; he admired everything about Mum.

Desks and chairs were lined up in uniform rows and Joseph and Isaac took their usual lucky exam seats, the two underneath the basketball post. Sitting anywhere else would be a bad sign.

A tall man with bushy sideburns and a blue stopwatch stood at the front and watched the other kids trickle in to the hall. Joseph kept his eyes down when he saw Pierre's spiky blond hair float through the door.

"Please take your seats!" the invigilator called. "The exam will be starting shortly."

Isaac swivelled in his chair and held out his fist. "Good luck."

Joseph returned the fist bump. "You too."

Silence descended over the hall as the invigilator clicked his stopwatch. "You have one hour. You may begin."

Joseph flipped over the paper to find a single question.

"*What does the ocean mean to you?*"

A collective inhale of breath signalled everyone's surprise. Was this it? One single question that determined whether they'd get to study with Dr Moray?

It was so ridiculous that Joseph chuckled. Obviously Dr Moray wouldn't ask standard questions about multicellular organisms or the migratory patterns of the European eel. Those answers were words to memorize from a textbook. Dr Moray wanted something that couldn't be revised.

"This can't be the test!" Pierre Crowfly stood up. Big, uncomfortable anger rippled across his rosy-cheeked face. "This is unfair! We demand another question!" He scanned the hall for an ally. "Oi, Nemo! You agree with me?"

Joseph didn't look up.

"Nemo," Pierre growled. "Tell them we want another question."

His pen shook in his hand, but Joseph stayed silent and kept his eyes on his paper.

Pierre slammed his hands against his desk.

"Crowfly, in your seat! Final warning or you'll be disqualified," the invigilator shouted. "This is Dr Moray's test. He's not interested in your intelligence. Just your curiosity."

Pierre grunted and sat back down. Joseph felt the bully's eyes burning into his skin, but he couldn't think about Pierre and his inevitable revenge. Joseph had to focus. He thought of what Mum had always told him and Flo. You couldn't study how to be curious. Curiosity was in your bones. Either you had it or you didn't.

Joseph began to write.

Chapter 6

THE STEALTHY PURSUIT OF A SUN HAT FULL OF SECRETS

By the time Mr Pilcher returned to his concierge cubbyhole, the lobby of the Fortunia was an explosion of noise. Flo and Funmi battled through the crowd of cameras searching for the woman with the green sun hat, but it was as though she had vanished. The voice that had relayed Mum's last message from *The Ariel* wasn't among the others that now fired questions at Flo like torpedoes.

"*Can you confirm when you last spoke to your mother, Florence?*"

"*Has Sir Frederick Titan been in touch?*"

"Stop!" Mr Pilcher stood atop his cubbyhole, a megaphone in hand. "All of you, out!"

The horde of journalists ignored the concierge's cries and continued to swarm through the lobby, now battling against some of the Fortunia residents who were trying to get to the door.

"Care to comment on the disappearance of Nellie Wanderday's boat?" Char Lamprey stuck her mic into Dame Varda's face.

"I do not care to comment," the old heiress replied. "Stop sensationalizing and leave these children alone! Out of my way before I set my hounds on you. I'm late for Pilates."

Flo edged towards the sanctuary of the palm trees and scanned the busy lobby from her vantage point, refusing to accept the woman was gone. Her eyes couldn't settle on any particular figure and finding the woman in such chaos felt impossible. That was until she saw Funmi burst from the unruly mob. She grabbed Flo's wrist and pulled her towards Mr Pilcher's cubbyhole. "I've found her!"

"Where?" Excitement sparked through Flo as she crouched low and crawled behind the cubbyhole. Funmi pointed ahead as a flicker of green disappeared round the corner into the elevator corridor. Flo's insides hiccupped. She nodded at Funmi and they jumped up, ignoring the shouts of the journalists as they raced away from the lobby.

Flo skidded round the corridor corner. The woman stood in front of the elevator at the end, her eyes fixed on the doors. She hadn't noticed them yet.

"Where's she going?" Funmi whispered.

"I don't know but we can't let her go!" The elevator pinged and Flo flapped her arms above her head. "Wait!" she called. "I need to talk to you. About my mum. Nellie Wanderday!"

The woman's head jerked like an electric shock. She looked towards Flo, the wide brim of her hat still covering her face.

"We can't talk here," the woman said. "They could be watching. Follow me if you want the truth." She stepped into the elevator and Flo ran towards the doors, but she wasn't fast enough to stop them closing. The downwards arrow flashed on the elevator panel.

"She's going to the basement," Funmi said. "What was she going on about? Who's watching us?"

"No idea." Flo gritted her teeth. Why was this woman acting so strangely? And what did she mean by the truth? "But no one knows the Fortunia better than us. We'll catch her up on the service stairs."

They ran along the maze of adjoining corridors until they reached the blue service door. Racing down the steps, they arrived at the bottom in record time. Funmi opened the door a crack and they peered into the basement. The underbelly of the Fortunia was an unloved place, with its scuffed wooden-panelled walls and peeling wallpaper. Fortunately, there was just enough light to illuminate the woman slipping through a set of double doors.

"The kitchen?" Flo and Funmi exchanged confused looks.

They crept past the chef's quarters, hoping Chef Arnaud wouldn't spot them. The dining room was for the elderly residents, but if the chef caught Flo and Funmi in his kitchen then their long-standing deal of getting dessert leftovers would be over before they could say tiramisu.

The stainless steel kitchen worktops were piled high with dirty plates from the morning's breakfast service. The shelves creaked with hundreds of glass jars full of brightly coloured spices and herbs.

"There's no other way out," Flo said. "She must be still in here."

Funmi checked her watch and crossed her arms.

"Chef will be coming to start prep on lunch soon. I'll keep a lookout."

Flo frantically searched through cupboards and opened oven doors. She checked the cold room, holding her nose as she wove round giant slabs of meat and boxes of frozen fish. The woman wasn't anywhere to be found and Flo kicked a crate of cheese in frustration.

Then came a clanging noise, so faint that Flo almost believed she'd imagined it. She emerged from the cold room and glanced at Funmi.

"Did you—?"

Funmi nodded.

They turned their heads towards the far corner of the kitchen. The pantry door was slightly ajar.

Flo raced across the tiles, knocking into the saucepans hanging from the ceiling. Anticipation made her clumsy, but she didn't care about the noise. She wanted to be loud, to show this woman that she was following.

Funmi reached the pantry first and yanked the door open. "I don't see her in here."

Flo stepped into the pantry, pushing large sacks and vegetable crates out of her way. She'd almost reached the back wall when she tripped and tumbled to the floor.

"You okay?" Funmi asked.

"Yeah." Flo rubbed her left wrist, evil-eyeing the crate of carrots that had brought her down. But where the crate had once been was now a gaping hole in the pantry floor. She peered down. It was dark and endless, and a cool breeze swept over her. "A tunnel," Flo whispered, awestruck.

"Has she gone down there?" Funmi crouched next to her.

"She must've." Flo clocked a ladder rung near the top of the hole. "How come we didn't know about this? I thought we'd explored every inch of the Fortunia."

"This place still has plenty of surprises up its sleeves." Funmi tied her braids up with a purple scrunchie. "We're going down there, aren't we?"

Staring into the dark tunnel, Flo thought of Mum. Although she didn't know what awaited her, Flo couldn't deny the tingle of excitement. Was this how Mum felt before every expedition? The scary but wondrous possibility of the unknown? Flo had lived through Mum's tales for so long that she'd never really thought about what it would be like to have one herself.

Flo nodded. "There's too many questions I need to ask this woman about Mum's last message to the coastguard. I need to find out what else she knows and who she's scared of. She's the only lead I have. If you don't want to come, I will absolutely, completely, totally understand."

"We're FSquared. Where you go, I go. And—"

"What you do, I do." Flo finished off their friendship pact, the one they'd created together on Funmi's fifth birthday.

With a deep breath, Flo stepped down and let the tunnel swallow her whole. Now she was an explorer, but she was not searching for undiscovered ocean creatures or scientific marvels.

She was in search of the truth.

Chapter 7

MEETING MARIANNE DE LA MER

The tunnel went so deep that Flo could no longer hear the hum of the city tram travelling back and forth above their heads. They had spent at least an hour navigating the sloping, twisting tunnel, and they still hadn't caught up with the woman.

"We must surely be halfway across Brinemouth by now." Flo spun round and shielded her eyes against the glare of the torchlight coming from Funmi's watch. "Mind my eyeballs!"

"My bad." Funmi tapped the screen and the bright light dimmed to a glow. "I made some modifications to the torch function, but I don't think I've got the brightness settings right."

"I'll say!" Flo rubbed her eyes until the yellow dots disappeared. "Does that fancy watch of yours have a compass? Can it tell us which direction we're going in?"

"Yup." Funmi tapped the screen again. "This tunnel is leading us north."

"Towards the coast," Flo muttered. "Why is the woman heading there?"

"Who knows? This is all so…weird." Funmi groaned as her trainers scuffed against the sloping floor.

"She's acting like someone with a lot of secrets." The tunnel veered a sharp left and Flo scraped her arm against the wall. "I just hope a few of them are about Mum."

There was a loud rumble and the ceiling vibrated. Loose chunks of crumbling rock began to fall. Flo grabbed Funmi's hand and dragged her through a shower of stone.

Flo's chest heaved through her coughs. She breathed out a cloud of dust like a wheezy dragon. "You okay?"

"No. I'm not okay." Funmi groaned as she brushed rock fragments from her hair. "This place is almost as bad as the Tunnel of Terrors!"

Flo shivered. Even the name of the scariest ride at the Aderemi Adventure Park filled her with fear. She thought of the metal carriage that had led her through a pitch-black tunnel, punctuated by howling screams and rotting smells, and how she'd felt the soft brush of mechanical fingertips against her face.

A loud crack, like an iceberg splitting in half, echoed down the tunnel. Flo jumped and squeezed Funmi's hand tighter. "What was that noise?"

Funmi squeezed back. "No idea, but we have to walk towards it."

The tunnel path narrowed, forcing them to twist their limbs like pretzels. They shuffled through gaps with their backs flat against the wall. Thankfully, it wasn't long until the path came to an end. Flo was less thankful to see it was a dead end.

"There has to be a way out." Funmi rallied. She swept her arm back and forth, the light from her watch searching for an exit.

"You're right." Flo thought of the dramatic news report that morning and how they'd made it sound like Mum and her crew had disappeared from the face of the earth. "Nobody just vanishes. That woman got out of this tunnel somehow. So will we."

Funmi kept the light steady as Flo checked every inch of every wall. She squeezed her hands through crevices in search of levers and secret door handles. She pushed against the tunnel wall in hope, but no part of it swung back revealing an escape. It stood firm, mocking her.

Flo was ready to give up when she felt something land on her hair. She ran her fingers through it, feeling grains of sand. She looked up and saw a square-shaped outline. The natural light was faint, but it seeped through the tunnel ceiling. Natural light meant one thing, Flo knew. They were close to the surface.

"Can you point the light higher?"

Funmi moved her hand and the torchlight illuminated a small brass-ring handle in the ceiling. "It's a trapdoor!"

"That must be where she went." The woman would've been tall enough to reach the handle, but Flo certainly wasn't. Not even on tiptoes. "Give me a boost."

Funmi braided her hands together and Flo stepped onto her palms. Her left hand scraped against the wall as she tried to balance.

"Make it quick!" Funmi huffed.

"Doing my best!" Balance found, Flo spread her hands wide. She drew her arms back and pushed upwards with all her might. Then came the same loud cracking noise they'd heard earlier and the ceiling groaned open.

More natural light poured into the tunnel and Flo punched the air in delight.

Funmi wheezed beneath her. “Could you celebrate when I’m not holding you up?”

“Sorry.” Flo grabbed onto the edge of the trapdoor and pulled herself through. She rolled onto her belly and dangled her arms back down. Funmi’s sweaty palms gripped her own and she pulled her through.

Kicking the trapdoor shut behind her, Flo finally looked up. It took a moment for her eyes to adjust to the light. When they did, she found herself in one of the old beach huts down on the seafront. The hut was small and smelled of saltwater. There was just enough space for a narrow bench next to the door with a porthole window.

“Flo.”

She spun around at the sound of Funmi’s voice. There, behind them, was the woman they’d been following sitting on a battered sunlounger in the corner of the hut.

“We found you!” Flo said. “Finally.”

“You were only ten minutes behind me.” The woman’s voice was smug. “Not bad at all. You’re quite the explorers.”

"Who are you?" Flo stepped forward and felt Funmi's hand on the back of her shirt.

The woman removed her hat to reveal long, black-blue hair that looked like seaweed. Freckles covered her round cheeks and her curious green eyes shone like emeralds in a sunken treasure chest.

"These disguises are going to kill me in this heat. Apologies for the goose chase, but I'm a wanted woman." She shrugged off a baggy green cardigan and a tattoo of a selkie peeped out of her T-shirt sleeve. "I'm Marianne de la Mer. It's a pleasure to meet you, Florence Cordelia Wanderday." She looked inquisitively at Funmi. "And you are?"

"I'm—"

Flo drew a finger to her lips. "Don't tell her your name too!" She was spooked as to how Marianne knew her unofficial middle name, the one that Mum and Dad had forgotten to put on her birth certificate. "Who are you, Marianne?" Flo asked again. "And what do you know about my mum's disappearance?"

"I have the answers you're desperately seeking. Trust me."

"Just a thought," Funmi said, "making us chase you doesn't exactly inspire trust."

A sad smirk flickered across Marianne's face. "I couldn't tell you back there. Some of the journalists are in Frederick Titan's pocket. He has people everywhere spying on his behalf. They'd do anything to protect him." She glanced at Flo. "But I knew you'd come after me. You're just like your mother. The two of us found that tunnel years ago when I lived at the Fortunia."

Questions darted around in Flo's head like a shark hunting prey. She didn't know which answers she wanted first. What did Mum's old boss, Frederick Titan, have to do with any of this? Why would he have people spying on Marianne?

"Nellie and I are old friends," Marianne added.

Flo frowned. "But Mum's never mentioned you."

Marianne bent forward and fiddled with her necklace. The familiarity almost winded Flo. The necklace was identical to Mum's golden locket. The clasp clicked open and Marianne held her locket up to the light. There was a picture of two girls on Brinemouth beach; they were young, but the likeness was clear.

"It's you and Mum," Flo whispered.

Marianne's eyes widened, as though rewatching memories. "My father was the architect of the Fortunia. It was boring living there at first, being the only kid.

When your mum arrived with her family, she and I became best mates. Things changed after Nellie was recruited to The Titans, though." Marianne pulled a tatty satchel out from under the sunlounger. She turned it upside down and notebooks fell out. "I'm an environmental journalist. Some people call me an activist like it's a bad word. There's nothing radical about protecting the natural world. We should all do it."

Marianne's hushed rage sounded just like Mum whenever she talked about protecting the oceans. The similarity shook Flo.

"I wanted to talk to you because Frederick Titan is not the hero you think he is," Marianne said. "I believe he is to blame for *The Ariel*'s disappearance."

"No." Flo's stomach lurched in disbelief. "That can't be right." Her legs wobbled and her body pulled her down onto the cold wooden floor of the beach hut. She couldn't imagine any version of Frederick Titan that would put Mum in danger.

"Sir Frederick is a good person." Funmi sat beside Flo. "He's helped so many people in Brinemouth and across the world. Teaching us how to better look after our planet."

"It's all a lie!" Marianne's face turned stormy and her eyes glared like a lightning bolt. "When Nellie first joined The Titans, she was so excited about being able to explore the world and its oceans. But with each trip, she noticed that Frederick would go missing, sometimes for days at a time, only to return with vague answers about where he'd been. The film cameras never followed him, so all anyone saw on *The Titans Tour* show was one big happy family doing good deeds for the earth.

"Your mum grew suspicious of him. When she told me about his disappearances during trips, I had to investigate. I was certain there was a story to uncover. But the deeper I got, the further your mum and I grew apart. I became obsessed with my work and there wasn't time for anything else. Not even friends." Marianne sniffed. "My investigation into Frederick Titan took me all over the world and it became *my* world."

"So how is all this connected to Mum's boat disappearing?" Flo was growing impatient, her mind swirling like a vortex. "None of what you're saying makes sense."

Marianne held up her hands. "Before you know the truth about the present, you must understand the past. I discovered that while Nellie, Percy and the rest of the experts in The Titans were protecting nature and helping communities, Frederick Titan had a hidden agenda. When he went missing during trips, he was buying up land and destroying natural habitats just so he could sell it on to developers for a profit. He'd steal local artefacts for museums and poach animals for collectors."

Flo's face twisted, the weight of everything Marianne had said pressing on her like a bruise. "That can't be the same man we watched every night on telly showing us the wonders of the natural world. It can't."

"I'm sorry. I take no pleasure in telling you this, but Frederick's deception runs deep," Marianne said, stifling a yawn. Flo noticed the dark circles and lines that ran underneath her eyes like rivulets. "When The Titans broke up after Percy's death, Nellie reached out to me again and I travelled back to Brinemouth. We both wanted to make things right, to expose Frederick together and show the world who he really is."

"If what you're saying is actually true, why didn't Mum tell us?" Flo demanded. "We shared everything! She wouldn't keep something so big from us."

"It had to be a secret. Your mum was scared about what might happen to your family if Frederick found out she was investigating him," Marianne said. "Over the last three years, we met in this beach hut in the early hours of most weekends. Nellie would take the tunnel from the Fortunia and we'd work together, following up sources and gathering more proof. Taking down a powerful, adored man like Frederick Titan is a long and difficult process."

Flo looked at Funmi, her best friend's gobsmacked face a mirror of her own. Flo wanted to speak, to shout, anything; but the words didn't come. The fear that had been circling her all day had finally caught up.

"I know this is a lot to take in," Marianne said. "But I believe it's the reason why your mum's boat is missing. She wasn't going to research deep-sea ecosystems. She was going to find the final piece of proof we needed to stop Frederick for good."

Chapter 8

THE ISLAND

Flo wasn't sure how many more secrets she could take. She felt herself expanding with them. "What was it? The final piece?"

"Three months ago we had a breakthrough." Marianne's voice was almost as faint as the waves outside. "I discovered that Linas, Frederick's right-hand man, had arranged an evening meeting in the Kelp Inn with a top scientist. I planted a listening device under the table. Turns out Linas was trying to recruit this scientist for Frederick's latest project. He didn't give any details except that they'd be joining a small team of other scientists, the best in their respective fields. The project would pay very well and it was taking place on a secret island somewhere in the North Atlantis Ocean. It immediately sounded suspicious."

Understanding settled over Flo. "Mum went to find the island, didn't she?"

Marianne's nod was heavy. "We both knew that a secret island was bad news. The things Frederick has done just off camera were bad enough, but an entire secret island? Recruiting scientists? We knew this project had to be dangerous. We had to find out what was happening."

"So why didn't you go with her?" Flo pushed. "Mum and her crew took all the risk!"

"We agreed that I'd stay here to monitor Frederick and keep digging for information, while they searched for the island." Marianne's expression remained calm. "She was going to film the journey and turn it into a documentary. That was our end goal and how we'd finally bring him down."

"Woah." Funmi whistled through her teeth. "That's a lot."

From Earth-hero to Climate-criminal, the treachery of Frederick Titan's double life was enough to make Flo's head spin. But finding out about Mum's covert investigation with Marianne, a secret island and a mysterious project; it all made Flo feel as though her head was going to fall clean off.

"Back at the Fortunia you said Mum's last message from *The Ariel* mentioned nine passengers," she said. "But Mum and her crew make eight. Do you think Frederick sent someone after her boat?"

Marianne nodded. "Nellie had been keeping in touch with me via radio too, but we'd fallen out of contact two days ago. When I intercepted the coastguard message and heard her say there were nine of them on board, I knew she was in trouble. That was our agreed code."

"I knew Mum wouldn't have made a mistake!" Flo cried. "It *was* an SOS message."

"Exactly." Marianne spoke faster now. "So either Frederick got wind of our investigation and sent someone to destroy her boat, or Nellie found the island and they were stopped before she could uncover what was going on."

"Destroy?" For the second time today, Flo's tears caught in her throat. "But they were friends! Even if everything you're saying is true, he wouldn't hurt Mum. Would he?"

Marianne looked down at her hands. "I can't be sure.

Frederick would do anything to protect the double life he's lived for so long."

"I— Flo's voice broke like a crumbling sea cliff. She felt Funmi's arms tighten round her and she sank into her best friend's hug.

"It's going to be okay," Funmi whispered. "Are you alright?"

"Of course," Flo sniffed. "I have to be."

"You don't have to be anything. I got you. Save the bravado for someone who believes it."

"It's not safe for us to be here much longer." Marianne's eyes glanced to the porthole window. "Frederick's spies are still looking for me. I have to get out of Brinemouth and find your mum."

"Wait!" Out of all Flo's mixed-up emotions burst an idea. It was wild, but it put a fierce wind in her sails. "I have to find her too. If you were investigating Frederick Titan, then we should carry on together. Let's follow Mum's journey across the ocean!"

"I'm used to working alone." Marianne pursed her lips. "People get in trouble around me."

"What happened to Mum isn't your fault." Flo's voice wobbled. "You both made a plan. But now I need one. I can't wait at home and do nothing."

Marianne shook her head and her long hair fell across her face. "It's too dangerous. Nellie would never forgive me if anything happened to you."

"So we just have to be extra careful," Flo continued. "You need us as much as we need you. You find a way for us to travel and we'll keep investigating Frederick. Maybe we can find out more about the island and this project of his."

"How do you plan on doing that?"

Flo and Funmi exchanged a glance.

"Eavesdropping," Funmi offered. "Frederick's spies, the journalists in his pockets. If they're hanging around the Fortunia, we can follow them and find out what they know. They'll be looking for you, but not us. We can be sneakier."

Flo nodded. "We'll use that to our advantage."

Marianne sprang up from the sunlounger. She seemed re-energized. "All I have are *The Ariel*'s coordinates from two days ago, when I last spoke to Nellie. She didn't know the island's exact location, so she was trying to cover as much of the North Atlantis as possible. That ocean isn't small. It won't be easy for us."

Flo met Marianne's eyes and held her gaze. "Since when is anything worth doing easy?"

Silence filled the tiny beach hut. Flo waited.

"Okay," Marianne said. "Great gills, I might regret this but we'll go together. I'll find a boat for us and we meet back here tonight. 10.30 p.m. I need to tie up some loose ends and that should give you enough time to try and find out anything else about Frederick's project."

Flo clasped her hands together. "Thank you." She was scared, but she no longer felt hopeless. You could achieve even the most impossible of things with a sliver of hope. Uncle Percy had taught her that.

"Come on," Funmi said. "Let's get back to the Fortunia."

"Yes." Marianne stuffed the notebooks back into her satchel and slung it over her shoulder. "I'll see you tonight. Be careful."

Flo and Funmi prised open the trapdoor and Flo lowered her friend back into the tunnel. She turned back to say goodbye, but heard only the sound of a sliding bolt and padlock clicking into place.

Marianne de la Mer was already gone.

Chapter 9

A PHOTOGRAPH AND AN INVITATION

"Wait up, Joe!"

Joseph saw Isaac sprinting towards him through Olde Brine Square, clutching a pink-and-white striped paper bag to his chest as he dodged tourists and street performers.

"Sorry," Joseph said once Isaac had caught up. "I had to get away from Pierre. Did you see his face when I ignored him?" He shuddered. "And I've got to get home. Flo might've found out something."

Isaac waved the paper bag under his nose. "Luckily for you, I thought I'd carry on our post-exam tradition. Dig in."

Joseph breathed in the sugary scent of Cousteau's

Confectionery and fished out a foam shrimp. Isaac slurped on a strawberry sea worm as they continued across the square.

"It's weird," Joseph said after another handful of shrimp. "I worried about that exam for months, but it doesn't seem important now. Nothing does until I hear from Mum."

Isaac patted him on the back, leaving sugary fingerprints on his shirt. "She and her crew will be fine. Your mum is tough. She was the only one who went up against my mum at resident meetings. Remember?"

Joseph smiled, remembering the intense debates their mums had got into. Whether it was about the Fortunia's fire policy or what colour to paint the hallways, they always had an opinion. Most meetings still ended with them chatting in the lounge, sharing a pot of tea and a plate of rugelach, home-made pastries filled with chocolate and raisins. Since Isaac's mum passed away four years ago, the Fortunia resident meetings were more subdued, missing the spark of Rose Kessler.

"I think your mum actually made Pilcher wee himself in fear once."

Isaac almost choked on his fifth strawberry sea worm.

"Great gills! I'd forgotten about that." His grin quickly vanished. "I wish I'd inherited her bravery."

"After what you did at school this morning," Joseph replied, "I'm pretty sure you have."

Isaac smiled shyly and returned to his pick 'n' mix.

Passing the fountain, Joseph looked up at the blue marble sculpture of Brinemouth's local heroes: Mum, Uncle Percy and Frederick Titan. Mum stood nestled between them, her long hair billowing in an invisible breeze as she held her camera – sculpted from copper – to her face. Reminders of Mum were everywhere in this city and although it usually made Joseph swell with pride, today he felt angry. Why did Mum have to be an explorer? The world was a dangerous place.

A flash of light suddenly swallowed his vision. When the blurry dots disappeared from his eyes, Joseph saw someone on the other side of the fountain with a camera in hand. They were dressed in a blue tracksuit and a navy cap was pulled over their face.

"Hey!" Joseph called. "What are you doing?" He ran towards them, but the person sprinted away and pushed through a crowd of tourists. Joseph tried to track their movements, but they were too quick and vanished from view.

"Did you see that?" Joseph looked back at Isaac. "That person took a picture of me!"

"It was probably one of those paparazzi from earlier." Isaac grimaced. "Trying to get a snap for the front page."

"Yeah, probably." Joseph noticed something on the ground and bent down to pick it up. The person had dropped a photograph and when he turned it over, Joseph almost dropped it again in shock.

"Look at this!" He waved it in Isaac's face. The photograph was of the entire Wanderday family the night before Mum had left for her expedition. They'd gone for dinner at the Kelp Inn and this photo had been taken just as they were leaving. Joseph had his arm looped through Mum's and Flo and Dad were play-fighting in the background.

Isaac pulled a face. "This is freaky."

"The person who took a photo of me just dropped this." Joseph's heartbeat pounded in his ears. "They must've been following me and my family around for weeks, in secret."

"But why? The news about your mum was only announced this morning. Normal paparazzi don't care about being seen. They wouldn't secretly follow you.

Plus, paparazzi take photos, they don't walk around with them in their pockets."

"I don't know why or what it means yet, but it can't be good." Joseph folded the photo and tucked it into his pocket, trying to ignore his queasy stomach. He thought of the video game he'd played with Flo last week at the arcade. They were both assassins and had been given a photograph of their targets. Was Joseph now a target?

"Let's get back home," Isaac said.

Their steps were heavy as they hurried through the cobblestoned streets that soon led to the main road. Joseph looked over his shoulder, expecting to see the person in blue reappear. He wasn't letting his overactive imagination get the better of him. The photograph in his pocket was proof.

Someone was watching the Wanderdays.

Five tiny dogs ran around the apartment hallway and Joseph groaned as he closed the door. The dogs meant that the Fortunia's most annoying resident was their latest babysitter. He prayed that Flo was already home. He had to show her the photograph and find out if she had any news about Mum. Plus, dealing with Dame

Varda required the strength of two people.

"Darlings! In here!"

Joseph headed to the movie room, dogs in tow, and found Dame Judi Varda wedged in Flo's beanbag. Her rainbow kaftan billowed out like a parachute.

"Joseph!" The ancient heiress flashed her lipstick grin, smudges of red stuck to her front teeth.

"Good afternoon, Dame Varda." Joseph smiled so hard his cheeks ached.

"We thought we'd come over early now that school's out for summer." Dame Varda shook the golden bangles on her wrists and the dogs whizzed to her side. "How are you holding up, angel?"

"I'm okay." Joseph lingered by the door, mentally calculating how fast he could escape to his bedroom.

"Glad to hear it. Chin up, petal." Dame Varda pointed to the other beanbag. "A letter came for you."

Joseph rushed towards it, his chest tightening. Was it an update about Mum? Had her boat been found?

The logo on the letter front stopped him in his tracks. He recognized the Greek god Poseidon rising from a sea of swirling waves. It was Sir Frederick Titan's trademark logo.

He ripped the letter open.

Dear Wanderdays,

I was most distressed to hear the news about Nellie and her crew. Although we haven't worked together in a long time, I've always thought of Nellie as family. Therefore, I would love to offer my extensive resources to help with the investigation of her boat's disappearance.

Please come and dine with me tonight at Titan Towers and we can discuss a plan of action to find The Ariel *and bring her home. A car will pick you up at half past six.*

Cordially,

Sir Frederick Titan

"Everything okay, sunshine?"

"It's Sir Frederick Titan," Joseph breathed out. "He's invited us to Titan Towers for dinner tonight. He wants to help find Mum's boat."

"Marvellous!" Dame Varda clapped and the movie room erupted with a chorus of enthusiastic barks. "If anyone can find your mother quicker than the police, it's Sir Frederick. Oh what a saint he is! You must feel better already."

Joseph pictured Frederick Titan's private fleet of helicopters and boats scanning the ocean for Mum. Maybe everything would be okay. Exhausted, he sunk into his beanbag. "Is Flo home?"

"Not yet," Dame Varda replied. "She and Funmi were messing about in the lobby earlier with a load of those journalists. Awful business. But if she's at the Aderemi's, she'll be home soon. How about we watch something until then?"

Joseph sighed as he reached for the remote. Flo and Funmi always got carried away together, but he was impatient to talk to his sister and tell her about the photograph. He'd found proof that someone had been watching his family before Mum went missing, and now he needed Flo's help to make sense of it all.

The screen flickered to life and a piano melody spilled through the speakers as a vast forest appeared. Joseph bristled. It was an episode of *The Titans Tour*, one that Joseph recognized immediately. The Titans had travelled to the Frondoso Forest to learn more about the indigenous community who lived in the treetops and to help them stop the deforestation threatening their home.

"Oh tides!" Dame Varda gasped. "They must be

showing this because of the news. I'm sorry, peach. Let's turn it over."

Joseph had seen this episode a hundred times before, normally with Flo or Mum and Dad. The usual comfort of the cinema room felt far away, but seeing Mum's freckled face on the screen stirred something in him. "No, it's okay. We can leave it on."

As Mum followed the Frondoso River out to the ocean, Joseph's mind wandered back to the last conversation he'd had with her before she'd left. They'd been in her studio and Joseph was helping her organize her film reels when she'd let out a huge sigh.

"What is it?" he'd asked.

"I'm getting tired, Jojo Bean. I don't think I have many more expeditions in me. I miss home too much."

"Don't go then."

"This is the most important trip of my life." Mum had ruffled his hair. "I have to go. When I'm back, I won't be going anywhere else without you. Promise."

Joseph would've done anything to hear Mum call him by his nickname now. He rubbed the side of his head as though he could smooth out this thought, but it refused to budge. He kept thinking about what Mum had said. *The most important trip of my life.* He felt silly for not asking her why. Why hadn't he asked her more questions when she'd been right here?

But maybe he could still find out why.

Chapter 10

A SOLO INVESTIGATION

Dame Varda's rasping snores soon filled the movie room and Joseph tiptoed past her snoozing dogs. Mum's studio had to hold answers about her latest trip and why it had been so important. He didn't need to wait for Flo, he could investigate all by himself.

Joseph shut the door to Mum's studio and started his search. The ceiling to floor bookshelves were stuffed full of research books and travel logs and he pulled them down, rooting through their contents. He scanned each page, but there was only information from previous research trips with old dates scribbled at the top. Open books soon covered the floor; a three-week observation log of an orca pod in the Magellan Ocean and a coastal trip itinerary to study kelp forests near the island of Ecklonia. Joseph went through every single detail, but none of it had anything to do with Mum's last trip.

He moved over to the mahogany desk that creaked under the weight of a dozen computer screens and video editing equipment. He searched through the desk drawers, only finding old receipts and one blue notebook. He flicked through pages containing scribbled charts and graphs, but none of them made sense.

Something sharp cut his finger and Joseph winced. There was a spiky bit of paper sticking out of the notebook's spine, like a page had been ripped out. Did that mean anything? Could there be a missing page that contained important information? He searched through the rubbish bin, but found nothing.

Joseph banged his fists against the desk and collapsed into the chair, feeling like the world's worst detective. He wanted to find a clue, but he'd just made a mess so far and, as his eyes scanned the desk, he realized he'd also broken one of Mum's favourite possessions.

The wonky model of the Aquarius Reef Base, a yellow oblong-shaped underwater laboratory, had fallen over and a thin crack ran down its middle. Joseph had made the model in art class last year for Mum. He picked it up, desperately hoping superglue would fix it, when a piece of paper fell out from its hollow base.

Joseph's hands couldn't move fast enough to unfold the paper. Was this the missing page from Mum's notebook? For once, he didn't linger on his thoughts. He just concentrated on the words written in Mum's scrawled handwriting.

My loves,

If you're reading this then I'm not home from my latest expedition and you've come in search of answers. It's possible that something bad has happened to me and my crew. We weren't going to explore deep-sea ecosystems. This trip was something else, something dangerous.

I'm sorry that I've kept you in the dark for so long. I thought I was keeping you all safe, but maybe I should've shared more.

Anyway, it's never too late for the truth. I think it might be the only thing that will save me if something goes wrong.

Find our home on the globe and you'll find the answers you need. Sorry for talking in riddles. I know your curiosity won't steer you wrong. I love you very much.

Mum xx

Joseph read the note again. Mum had lied about her trip and gone after something *dangerous*. Thoughts and feelings tangled up inside him like a fishing net, but he willed his imagination not to run away with a thousand terrible scenarios. He had to focus on the facts. The note was real. He had to follow Mum's instructions.

Joseph hurried over to the gigantic globe rising out of the floor in the corner of the studio. It was carved from glossy walnut wood and had always looked like something that belonged in a museum. He circled the globe, tracing his fingers across its smooth surface until he found his home city.

When his fingers landed on Brinemouth, something felt different. The globe wasn't smooth here. The carving of Brinemouth was raised, jutting ever so slightly out from the globe. He pressed down and Brinemouth receded into the wood. Joseph jumped back as the top of the globe whirred and split in half like an Easter egg. When the noise finally stopped, he crept forward and peered into the open globe to find a metal ladder leading down through a hole. Intrigue sucked him in like a whirlpool.

There was a hidden passageway in Mum's studio and the discovery excited and scared him in equal measure. The answers about her latest trip were right under his feet and he prayed they'd help him figure out how to find Mum and her crew. If he could find out why the trip had been dangerous, maybe he could find out what had gone wrong and how to rescue them.

He gripped the ladder and began his descent. The air was thick with dust and it tickled his nose, but he carried on through the darkness. When his feet reached solid ground, a wall light flickered on. He was in a hallway that he'd never seen before. It was just like every other hallway in the Fortunia, except that this one had damp walls and broken floorboards.

Where was he? Still in their apartment or on an abandoned floor of the Fortunia that only Mum knew about? Either way, her note had led him down here. He had to carry on.

As he neared the end of the hallway, a single wooden door came into view. Joseph hesitated, almost tripping as a mouse skittered across the floor, but then he reached for the doorknob and turned it. His fingers tingled with nervous anticipation.

Opening the door felt like discovering hidden treasure. This kind of excitement was a new feeling for him. Now he was an explorer just like Mum.

Joseph stepped through the door and into a room, his mouth dropping open when he saw what was inside.

Mum's secret wasn't little. It was so big it required a whole room.

Somewhere above Joseph's head, a door slammed shut. The sound of his sister calling his name snapped him out of his stupor.

Flo was home.

Just wait until he showed her what he'd found.

Chapter 11

HOME TRUTHS IN THE HIDDEN OFFICE

The hidden room that Joseph had discovered looked like an office from a detective movie and Flo struggled to take everything in. There was a giant corkboard full of newspaper clippings and photographs of animals and natural disasters. Another wall was plastered with maps. Small red pins were dotted all over the vast blue of the world's oceans. A desk and velvet sofa were covered with papers and stacks of books. It was as though Mum had dumped every single thought she'd had into this room.

"I've not looked through any of it yet." Joseph's fingers twitched at his side. "But there's got to be something down here that will tell us where Mum was actually going."

Flo didn't mean to ignore her brother, but the discovery of this hidden room overwhelmed her and she rushed forward without answering. "This must be where she kept all her research into Frederick and the island too," she said. "If only we'd found this place sooner. If only she'd told us what she knew! We could've helped Mum and Marianne with their investigation!"

"What are you talking about? Who is Marianne?" Joseph's hand on Flo's shoulder stopped her in her tracks. "What do you know that I don't?"

His touch brought Flo back to reality. "Sorry, bro." Her brain quickly arranged everything she needed to tell him in the right order: the truth about Frederick Titan, Mum and Marianne's investigations, the island and the mysterious project. She guided Joseph over to the sofa. "I already know the truth about what Mum was really doing on her latest trip. I'll tell you everything. But first I think you better sit down."

Flo waited for Joseph to speak. She held his hand as he hunched forward on the sofa. It's no surprise he felt winded. Everything Flo had told him had taken the breath from her earlier.

"Do you really think it's true?" Joseph's voice was a whisper. "Everything Marianne told you?"

Flo nodded. "I do."

Joseph rustled in his pocket and thrust a photo at her. "Here."

"What's this?" Flo bristled at the sight of her own face staring back at her.

"Someone followed me and Isaac home from school. They dropped this photo when I chased after them. It's proof that someone's been following our family for weeks. I didn't get a good look at them, but after everything you just told me…you reckon it was likely one of Frederick Titan's *spies*?"

"I know how it sounds, but he's a powerful man. He pays people silly amounts to work for him and in return they keep quiet about his true self." Flo shrugged. "Money talks."

"But you've only just met Marianne." Joseph's voice was strained. "We've known Frederick longer. She could be the one lying!"

Flo knew Joseph would take some convincing. He wasn't ready to admit that Frederick Titan, one of his heroes, could be a bad person. "I'll show you it's the truth." She took his hand and led him over to the map on the far wall. It had caught her eye earlier, the purposeful pattern of the tiny flag pins.

"Mum pinned every single location they travelled to during *The Titans Tour*. There's notes next to every location that correspond to episodes they filmed. Listen to this." Flo tugged a Post-it free. "*Episode 15. While we worked to restore the mangrove forests protecting the coast of Gadamascar, Frederick met with the CEO of a palm-oil company. Marianne discovered that, during this meeting, Frederick was paid seven figures to later return to Gadamascar and destroy our newly planted forest and make space for a new palm-oil plantation.*"

Joseph let out a noise, half-hiccup, half-sob.

"And another one." Flo read from a second Post-it. "*Episode 30. The Titans created a new animal sanctuary for endangered black rhinos in South Bamin. A week later the sanctuary was raided by poachers. Earlier this year, I traced the money from the sale of two rhino horns from that sanctuary to one of Frederick's offshore bank accounts. He had organized the raid and sold the horns for a hefty profit.*"

Flo looked at Joseph just in time for her brother to fall against her. She hugged him tight. "I'm sorry. I know how much you looked up to him."

They stood like that, each other's anchors in the worsening storm.

"A letter came earlier." Joseph sniffed and wiped his nose. "From Frederick. He's invited us to dinner tonight at Titan Towers. He wants to help us find Mum. I thought it was a good thing. But now – what are we going to do? Is it a trap? Maybe we should wait until Dad's home tomorrow morning. He'll know what to do."

Flo felt two things bloom inside her. Fear that Joseph was right, and the invitation was a trap. And fear that, if Frederick was responsible for Mum's boat going missing, he might want to make the rest of the Wanderdays disappear too! But Flo also felt hopeful. Frederick had given them the perfect opportunity to snoop round his house and to find the one thing they needed before setting off in search of Mum themselves.

"We've got to go," Flo said, decidedly. "It could be our only chance to find the coordinates to the secret island. All of this," she pointed to each wall, "doesn't feel like a coincidence. Mum was investigating Frederick Titan and now she's missing in the same ocean where his island is. Finding the coordinates gives us a chance to find Mum and her crew. We can't wait for Dad to get home. We have to act now."

"But what if we get caught?" Joseph winced. "It's too risky!"

One of Uncle Percy's favourite sayings popped immediately into Flo's head.

"Everything in life is a risk, kid," she said. "So you can sit on the sidelines or you can..."

"...jump right in and play with everything you've got." A smile reappeared on Joseph's face. Uncle Percy's words always had a calming effect on her brother. Even though he was no longer around, Flo could count on her uncle's back catalogue of cheesy motivational quotes to inspire Joseph.

He hurried over to the desk in the corner of the room. "We better crack on down here before Dame Varda wakes up."

Joseph's eagerness took Flo by surprise, but she welcomed it. "You go through the files on the desk and I'll look at all the corkboards," she said. "Keep an eye out for anything that mentions islands in the North Atlantis Ocean or *The Ariel*'s navigation route."

Joseph nodded. "Got it."

Flo started scanning each wall, studying Mum's scribbled notes and following the lines on the maps drawn from one location to another. There was plenty of evidence about Frederick Titan's deceitful behaviour during his time as leader of The Titans, but nothing seemed to link to Mum's latest trip. Flo peeled back layers of documents, her frustration growing, until she found a smaller map of the Atlantis Ocean. There was a big red X marked at the top. Flo stepped closer to decipher Mum's tiny, scribbled writing next to it.

PP boat last sighted here three years ago

What did PP stand for? Flo unpinned the map from the corkboard and searched through the mess of information, hoping for something that would reveal its meaning.

A photograph, torn at its edges, stopped Flo in her tracks. It was a picture of Mum and Uncle Percy standing on Brinemouth Pier. At the bottom Mum had scribbled another note.

Last known pic of Percy Parish. Taken before his final voyage in the North Atlantis. Considered lost at sea, but no boat or body was ever found.

"Uncle Percy," Flo whispered to herself. "Percy Parish. That's what PP stands for!"

Why had Mum marked the last sighting of Percy's boat on this map? Uncle Percy had died three years ago and Flo's memories of him were beginning to break apart like driftwood. She could no longer remember his favourite ice-cream flavour or how many times they'd ridden the helter-skelter on Brinemouth Pier. Flo looked at the photograph, then back at the map. Uncle Percy's boat was last sighted in the North Atlantis. Now Mum's boat had gone missing in the same area of the ocean. Confusion swirled inside Flo like a maelstrom; the depth of discovery was growing larger and larger.

"Any luck?" Joseph's voice made Flo jump. "I didn't find anything that mentioned the island or *The Ariel*'s route on her desk. But it looks like she was in the process of turning all her research on Frederick Titan into a documentary script." His bottom lip quivered. "It's scary how wrong you can be about a person."

"I know." Flo sensed her brother's imminent spiral and she pointed at the photograph and map she'd found. "But check this out. Uncle Percy's sailing accident happened in the same area where Mum's boat has gone missing."

"Huh?" Joseph frowned. "Why was Mum looking into that?"

There were a hundred questions gathering speed and Flo didn't know which direction to take them. "I've got no idea. But here's what I do know. We'll go to Titan Towers and we *will* find the island coordinates. We'll cross the ocean, find Mum and her crew, and bring them home."

Joseph sniffed. "Can we really do all that?"

"Of course!" Flo said. "We're Wanderdays. We're not afraid of going to new places. And there's nothing we wouldn't do for the people we love, right?"

Flo watched Joseph's face wrestle with opposing emotions. "You're sure we shouldn't wait for Dad? Even if we do find the island coordinates tonight, couldn't we wait until tomorrow to set off, when he's back?"

Flo shook her head. "Each minute that ticks by is another minute that we're not out there looking for Mum. I don't like it either, but every second counts. We'll leave a note for Dad explaining everything." She thought of the endless expanse of the ocean. "But no one is going to search for Mum as hard as we will. You get that, right?"

"I do," Joseph whispered. "I'm just scared."

Despite the undeniable fear, Flo could also see the resolve on her brother's face; an understanding that he would do anything and go anywhere to get Mum back.

"You know something," Flo said, "Mum once told me she was scared each time she went on an expedition. She just never wanted to let her fear get in the way of doing something important and making a difference."

"Really?" Joseph's face lifted in surprise. "I thought she was always brave. Just like you." His stomach rumbled with the force of a train. "Sorry. I only had sweets for lunch."

Flo laughed. "We'll get a snack before we head to dinner." She thought of Titan Towers, Frederick Titan's home sitting atop the highest hill in Brinemouth, and how the island coordinates had to be hidden somewhere inside his sprawling mansion. "Plus, I'm not *always* brave. No one is all the time. That would be exhausting."

Flo looped her arm through Joseph's and pulled away from Mum's hidden office and towards a new secret plan of their own.

Chapter 12

THE PLUS ONES AND THE PLAN

"This is unbelievable. Take something the average amount of unbelievable, like aliens landing in Brinemouth, times it by a billion and it still wouldn't even come close to how unbelievable this is!"

Isaac paced back and forth in Joseph's bedroom, stepping over the piles of clothes that Joseph still hadn't tidied away. He and Flo had called their best friends after emerging from Mum's secret office. They couldn't go to Titan Towers all alone; if they were going to sneak away to search for the island coordinates, they'd need a distraction. Or two.

"Frederick Titan is a god around here." Isaac fiddled with his Hamsa necklace; he'd never once taken off the last birthday gift from his mum. "This could change everything. But do you really think he'd put your mum in danger?"

Joseph had tried hard to not let his thoughts get the better of him, but now all the terrible potential scenarios shot out of his brain like black ink from a panicked octopus: Frederick Titan giving orders to his spies to sabotage *The Ariel*; Mum and her crew overboard, struggling to stay afloat and alive in the unpredictable waters. He rubbed his temple, wishing for it all to stop.

"I didn't want to believe it at first," he said, glancing over at Frederick's sparkling grin on The Titans' poster. "But I believe Mum and everything she's investigated. The Frederick Titan that the world knows is a mask he hides behind. Who knows what he'd do to keep it that way?"

Joseph's bedroom door creaked open and in came Flo and Funmi, holding four chipped mugs between them.

"Your favourite." Flo handed Joseph a mug. "Iced chocolate with a sprinkling of the finest sea salt from Seaport salt marsh. Even Dame Varda wanted one, but she'd fallen asleep again by the time I made hers!"

Joseph took a sip and felt the cold sweetness of the

iced chocolate slide down his throat. The summers were warm, but they'd grown hotter as each year had passed without any real attempt from any government to reduce the global temperature. He and Flo had invented the iced chocolate last summer, setting up a stand in Plankton Park to sell their refreshing drink and raise money for Brinemouth's "Better World" charity.

"Right." Flo slurped from her mug and sat down in the octopus-shaped desk chair. "Have you filled Isaac in?"

Joseph nodded. "He's up to speed with everything you and Funmi found out from Marianne. As well as the stuff we found in Mum's office."

"Great." Flo set her drink on the desk and stretched her fingers. "So on to our plan: finding the island coordinates at Titan Towers."

"I saw Titan Towers when Frederick was doing an interview on the TV." Funmi kicked off her shoes and bellyflopped onto the bed next to Joseph. "That place is a fortress. There's four levels and over fifty different rooms."

"That's a lot of snooping to cover in just one evening." Isaac's face reminded Joseph of a wise owl. "How will we know where to look?"

"We visited once with Mum and Dad, but it was years ago. Just after Uncle Percy died, so my memory's a bit hazy." Flo's forehead crinkled. "Frederick took us on a tour of the place. You were desperate to see his library. Do you remember anything, Jojo?"

Joseph closed his eyes and pictured Titan Towers in his mind: the grand glass foyer they'd walked through, the smell of paper and dust in the library and all the wooden doors that opened into beautiful bedrooms, porcelain bathrooms, and sitting rooms. He saw a spiralling staircase with narrow stone steps behind a curtain and a small window that looked out over the city, the ocean like a thin blue line beyond it. Then a corridor at the top of the steps. And at the end of that, a locked door.

"There was a locked door in the turret." Despite his mind always trying to trip him up, Joseph's memory held solid. "I remember thinking it was weird because he wouldn't take us in there and he'd shown us every other room. Dad joked about there being some sort of three-headed monster behind the door."

"Nice one." Isaac raised his mug of iced chocolate. "That's got to be worth exploring."

"I can't remember the way up to the turret, though,"

Joseph replied. "The house was so big."

"Well it's got to be a good place to start our search," Flo smiled. "Well remembered, Jojo."

Funmi raised her hand. "I've got a question."

Flo nodded. "Go on."

"When are you actually going to get the chance to sneak away during dinner?"

"That's where both of you come in," Flo replied. "Will you come with us tonight? You could distract Frederick while we sneak away to search the turret."

"Obviously." Funmi grinned. "Like you were ever going without me."

"But what if we get caught? Your parents will freak out!" Joseph pictured the morning news headline already: DAUGHTER OF BRINEMOUTH'S TOP THEME PARK OWNERS ARRESTED FOR STEALING FROM TITAN TOWERS. PARENTS SAY WANDERDAY KIDS A BAD INFLUENCE.

"I don't want to sit this out just because it's bad for their *business*." Funmi said the word like a curse. "I just want to be me. Not the perfect daughter they expect all the time. I'm doing this, no matter what happens."

"And my dad won't even notice that I'm not at home tonight." Isaac shrugged. "He barely notices me at all."

"That's not true."

Isaac shrugged at Joseph. "Trust me. All he does is work. Since—" He trailed off, his hands reaching for his necklace. "I could bring my ladybird collection to Titan Towers! That'll entertain Frederick for ages."

"Flo said to distract him, not send him to sleep," Funmi groaned, throwing a pillow at Isaac. "The key to distracting Frederick Titan is getting him to talk about himself. Old guys like him love talking about their glory days."

"But—" Joseph thought of his run-in with the person in blue earlier. If Frederick's spies had been watching his family's every move for weeks, how could Flo expect them to waltz right into Titan Towers and take what they needed?

"Go on, what is it?" Flo asked.

"Titan Towers will be full of security. Not just guards, but cameras and who knows what else. Frederick is rich enough to have the latest technology. There'll be eyes on us everywhere."

Flo downed the rest of her drink and wiped foam from her top lip. "We'll find a way, I'm sure."

"You can't be sure of anything!" Joseph shouted. "Frederick isn't the good person we thought he was.

This isn't like finding a secret tunnel in the Fortunia or discovering Mum's hidden office. This is sneaking around a man's house who might've hurt Mum! Who might hurt us!" His bedroom felt like a furnace and a sharp pain split across his head. Joseph stumbled over to the window and pushed it open.

"It's alright." He felt Isaac's arm on his shoulder guiding him back to the edge of his bed. "Just breathe." They sat together and Joseph rested his head between his knees, taking deep breaths until his head didn't feel as tight. When he looked up, Flo was sitting on the carpet in front of him.

"I'm sorry." She squeezed his knee. "You're right. I don't know what's going to happen at Titan Towers. I can't be sure of anything and I can't guarantee it will be easy. I'm just trying to be positive, Jojo. It helps me."

A silence fell over the bedroom as the four friends faced the truth of the matter: nothing about this was certain. The list of things that could go wrong seemed endless.

"I've got an idea!" Funmi jumped up from the bed. "Let's ask Frederick Titan for a tour. He clearly loves showing off his home and all the fancy things inside it. If he takes us on a tour before dinner, we can scope out the place. Get an idea of where the cameras are and anything else."

"That's a good idea," Joseph sniffed. "Actually, really good. If he shows us round we can double-check the entrance to the turret room too."

Funmi held up her palm to Flo. "Nailed it!"

Flo high-fived her best friend before turning back to Joseph. There was a big grin on his sister's face. "I've just remembered that there is one thing I'm sure of."

"What is it?"

Flo grinned. "I'm sure that as long as we're all in this together, we're going to be okay."

"Exactly." Isaac swung his arm round Joseph's shoulders. "So shall we put our hands together and shout 'GO TEAM'?"

Funmi groaned as loud as a humpback whale and the others burst into laughter.

Joseph felt his mind ease. There was so much uncertainty ahead, but they would face it together. His head clear, he stood up. "The car is coming in less than an hour to pick us up. We need to get ready."

"True." Flo looked down at her creased school shirt. "We'll get changed, get everything we need, and meet back here just before half six. Okay?"

With the plan made, everyone emptied out of Joseph's bedroom. He needed to trawl through his clothes to find something to wear, but a longing pulled him back over to the window. Every part of the city that made Brinemouth whole glistened in the sunshine like an iridescent pearl. And on the horizon was the sea, the endless expanse of water merging into the ocean and beyond.

"We're coming to get you, Mum." He pushed his hands through the gap in the window, as though he could send his words far across the ocean and they would find her.

Wherever she was.

Recording #1:

JOURNEY TO FANTOME ISLAND

It's 6.20 p.m. on 20th July and I'm recording this in my bedroom.

It's probably no surprise that I want to follow in Mum's footsteps and become a film-maker. Ever since she and Dad bought me this camera for my sixth birthday, it's become a third arm. It's always with me, so I can be ready to capture the parts of life that interest me most.

Mum started making films because she wanted to show everyone the importance of our oceans and how crucial they are to our survival.

Well, I want to make this film to show everyone the truth. The truth about the journey that me, Flo Wanderday, my brother Joseph and our best friends Isaac Kessler and Funmi Aderemi, are about to go on.

Let me share with you what we've uncovered so far.

We met Marianne de la Mer, an investigative journalist, ocean activist, and Mum's oldest friend. I think we're sort of friends now too. After The Titans broke up Mum and Marianne investigated Frederick Titan in secret together, gathering the evidence that they'd need to expose him once and for all.

Because he is no hero. He has contributed to and profited from the climate crisis, destroying our oceans and lands in order to make more money than one man needs. He is no protector of the natural world. He has always used it for his own gain. I reckon he considers himself more important than the planet we all live on, so yes, the Frederick Titan that the world knows is an imposter.

Mum's latest expedition was not the trip we thought she was going on. In fact, Mum and her crew went to locate a secret island owned by Frederick Titan, to find out what his next "project" is. The island is somewhere in the North Atlantis Ocean, which is the same part of the ocean where The Ariel *was last tracked. We don't know whether Mum found the island or something happened to her boat before they arrived. That is what we need to find out.*

So tonight we're going to Titan Towers to find the island coordinates. We intend to steal from under the nose of

Frederick Titan himself and find out whether he sabotaged Mum's journey to keep his secrets safe.

But we won't do this alone. Once we have the coordinates, we will meet Marianne de la Mer back at the beach hut at ten-thirty tonight. She is as determined as us to find Mum and make things right.

So I'm taking my camera along with us for the journey.

I have a feeling I won't believe the things I'll see unless I get them on film.

Chapter 13

THE TRIP TO TITAN TOWERS

At exactly half-past six the phone in the hallway rang. Flo knew it was coming, but it still made her jump.

"Your ride is waiting outside." Mr Pilcher's voice crackled down the line. "Quite fancy too. You better hurry."

"Joseph!" Flo slammed the phone down. "It's time to go."

He stepped out from his bedroom, dressed in a crisp white shirt and black trousers. His blue bow tie, illustrated with shells, was skew-whiff. "How do I look?"

"As sharp as piranha teeth, bro." Flo tugged at her trusty blue jumpsuit; its deep pockets provided plenty of space for extra camera batteries.

Joseph blushed. "Dad called while you were getting ready. You must not have heard it."

Flo adjusted the camera straps round her neck. "I was filming. Everything okay?"

"He's worried about us." Joseph looked down at his shoes. "He's trying to sound strong, but I know he's scared for Mum. I think he feels guilty he's not here while this is going on."

"You didn't say anything about our plan, did you?"

"Of course not!" Joseph squeaked with outrage. "I felt guilty about lying, though."

Flo had dealt with her own guilt by not thinking about Dad's face when he finally returned home and discovered they were gone. It had worked until now.

"I do too," she said. "But you know he would never let us go if he knew about our plan."

The doorbell chimed and Flo hurried to answer it. Opening the door, she was met with quite a sight. Isaac was still wearing his school shorts, but had added a crinkled, blue-striped shirt and appeared to have brushed his hair for the first time in months. And Funmi. Her best friend was in a dress that made Flo think of a sea urchin. Blue and purple tassels shot out of it like spikes.

"Don't ask." Funmi huffed. "Ameyo was home and insisted I borrow this. Said I had to make an effort for Titan Towers. Sisters are the worst. No offence."

"Oh, darlings!" Dame Varda's voice echoed in the hallway. Flo had almost forgotten the heiress was still there. Her babysitting had comprised of multiple naps. "You all look simply divine! Be on your best behaviour for Sir Frederick now, won't you?" Dame Varda grabbed Joseph and planted a sloppy kiss on his cheek. "It's not every day you get invited into a hero's home."

Flo nodded tightly. "We will." She ushered Joseph towards the door before he was attacked with another kiss.

Isaac pointed at a red smudge on Joseph's cheek. "You got a little something—"

"Yup." Joseph wiped his face with the back of his hand, his cheeks turning as red as Dame Varda's lipstick.

As she led the others through the courtyard, Flo spotted Ms Keoghan from 7C knitting underneath the elm tree.

"How are you holding up, my lovelies?" the retired dressmaker called. "I'm knitting you gifts. Thought they'd cheer you up."

"Thanks, Ms Keoghan," Flo replied, quickening her footsteps. "I'm sorry, but we can't stop!"

"Oh yes." She waved her needles. "Your carriage to Titan Towers awaits!"

"News travels fast in this place," Joseph muttered.

Flo pulled the gates open. "All the more reason to keep our plan top secret."

On the other side of the Fortunia gates was a sleek black limousine. Its huge silver wheels sparkled in the evening sun. The sunroof was open and delicate classical music wafted into the evening sky.

Funmi whistled. "Nice ride."

Flo beckoned the others into a huddle on the pavement. "Remember that this isn't a fun dinner. Frederick Titan has been watching our family for weeks." She glanced at Joseph. "We don't know what we're about to walk into, so be careful and don't give anything away. Okay?"

"Got it," Isaac whispered.

They broke apart just as the limousine front door swung open. A tall man dressed in a sharp blue suit with blond slicked-back hair appeared on the pavement.

"Good evening, Wanderdays! My name is Linas, Sir Titan's assistant." He bowed awkwardly before his eyes settled on the four of them. "Ah. You seem to have multiplied."

"We wanted to bring our best friends as our dad is away," Flo said. "Will that be a problem?"

"No, of course not!" Linas's steely voice made it sound like a problem. "I'll just let Cook know that there'll be four of you." He opened the passenger door. "Do make yourselves comfortable."

They crammed into the back of the limo. A blue mini fridge hummed between the plush leather seats.

"Help yourselves to snacks, but don't spoil your appetite." Linas winked, before the screen that separated the front and back seats whirred shut.

As tempting as the sweet treats were, Flo didn't reach for a coconut ice. None of them did. Frederick Titan had spent a lifetime showing off his kindness and generosity to the world, but now she knew that it had all been a lie, Flo couldn't let herself relax.

The limo wove its way through Brinemouth city centre and Flo winced as they bounced over cobblestone streets. Her city was not made for modern things. She and Funmi looked out of the window, as the limo crossed over the bridge, at the sprawling green of Plankton Park.

"Look at that." Funmi pointed to the tip of the

Wanderday Institute poking over the trees. "They've lit it up for your mum and her crew."

Flo drew her eyes up, making out the green and red lights twinkling around the dome in the early evening sky. They were the colours of *The Ariel.* She choked back a sob.

"It won't be like that for long," Funmi said. "The only lights we'll need will be for your mum's welcome home party."

Flo smiled, imagining Mum's awkwardness faced with a party thrown in her honour.

The city landscape soon fell away. The sprawling suburban houses and pastel-coloured shopfronts were replaced by rolling hills and the forest beyond. Wild flowers crept onto the edge of the busy motorway. The limousine drove straight for a while before turning off at an exit and Flo slid in her seat from the sharp turn.

"Are we here already?" Joseph asked.

They'd pulled up alongside a grassy bank. On the other side cars sped by in a blur.

"No," Flo replied. "Then why have we—?"

A whirring noise interrupted her. The trees on the bank moved apart like curtains and a thick bush, as tall as the limousine, shrunk into the ground. The engine growled and the limousine drove slowly through the space where the bush had just been. On the other side of the fake forest wall was a smooth tarmac road.

"A secret road to Titan Towers." Flo looked at her brother, her mouth a perfect O. "I don't remember this being here when we visited with Mum and Dad. Do you?"

Joseph shook his head. "We didn't come this way."

Flo thought of the tunnels underneath the Fortunia that led to the beach hut and Mum's hidden office; different forbidden places that seemed to hide mystery after mystery. Everyone had secrets; some were just worse than others. Flo wondered what terrible secrets would await them at Titan Towers.

"Look!" Isaac shouted. "There it is!"

Titan Towers was perched on the highest hill in Brinemouth. A low brick wall wrapped round the huge house. Not a house, but a fortress. That was the best word Flo could find. Palm trees stretched towards the clouds and a golden helicopter was parked on the rooftop helipad. Water from an infinity pool cascaded over the hill edge and merged into a waterfall below.

Frederick Titan was a very public person and never missed an occasion on Brinemouth's social calendar, from the opening of the new aquarium to charity fundraisers. But few people had ever actually been invited to Titan Towers, his private paradise. Flo wondered whether that was because of what was hiding inside.

"It looks even bigger than it did on the telly!" Funmi pressed her nose up to the window.

As the limousine continued its path up the hill, Flo trained her camera on Titan Towers. She zoomed in on the turret. It looked so high! Sneaking up there would feel like breaking into the clouds. But if that was what they had to do then so be it. Flo had told Marianne that they'd find the island coordinates. She couldn't let her down. She couldn't let Mum down.

The limousine navigated a final bend and pulled up outside towering golden gates. The front window wound down and a white camera swivelled towards the driving seat.

"*Face recognized,*" an automatic voice said as the gates swung open. "*Welcome to Titan Towers, home to Earth-hero Sir Frederick Titan.*"

"We'll see about that," Flo said, mouse quiet. The limousine drove past the security camera and the gates shut behind them with a metallic clunk.

There was no turning back.

Chapter 14

A DIFFERENT TYPE OF TITAN TOUR

Joseph wiped his sweaty palms on his trousers and tried to ignore his heart thudding against his skin. Could such an intense feeling actually break through his chest and explode? It felt possible.

"I'm panicking." He turned to Flo, his trousers squeaking against the leather sofa.

Linas had led the four friends through to the reception room where they'd been instructed to wait. The room was like a greenhouse, its glass windows trapping the heat inside. Despite the ice-cold breeze that blasted from the air con, Joseph felt sticky all over. Racing thoughts clung to every edge of his mind. The security camera on the wall certainly didn't help.

"Just focus on yourself," Flo whispered. "One breath after another."

"I've got something that might help our plan." Next to Joseph, Isaac patted his shorts pocket. "I swiped a key card from Linas earlier. He used it to open the main door and the reception door, so I'm thinking it's a master card. It might open every door in this place."

"How did you manage *that*?"

Joseph could tell Flo was trying not to look impressed with Isaac, but her tone betrayed her.

"My mum always said I have gentle hands." Isaac blushed. "They're the hands of an entomologist. Makes it easier to pick up beetles and bugs. And to swipe things, apparently."

Funmi patted him on the back. "Didn't think you had it in you."

Isaac grinned triumphantly. "Turns out I'm learning a lot about myself today."

The tightness in Joseph's chest relaxed. The prospect of sneaking into the turret room had him on edge, but Isaac's derring-do had emboldened him. And hadn't he also proved himself capable of things he'd never imagined? Today was a day of firsts.

"Good evening, Wanderdays and co!"

Frederick Titan's voice boomed around the reception room. Suddenly he was there, walking towards them with his arms outstretched in a half-prayer, half-hug. Joseph stifled a gasp at how different Frederick looked since the last time they'd seen him, at Uncle Percy's funeral. Now his hair was bright white and bushy sideburns trailed down to his earlobes, which sprouted bunches of white hair like cauliflower bunches.

Joseph stayed rooted to his seat, but Flo stood and offered a handshake. "Good evening, Sir Frederick. Thank you for inviting us."

"Please, just call me Frederick." He waved away Flo's hand. "It's the very least I could do. And I'm delighted that you brought your friends with you. There's strength in company during tough times, isn't there?"

"I'm Isaac Kessler." Isaac did a half bow.

"And I'm—"

"Funmi Aderemi." Frederick clapped his hands. "Of course I recognize you. Your parents are industrious folk. The adventure park has done wonderful things for Brinemouth. Just like myself, of course." His eyes moved on to Joseph; he was the only one still sitting. "And the youngest Wanderday! It's good to see you again, boy."

Joseph noticed the wrinkles and liver spots that

covered Titan's hands. In his head, Frederick Titan was a figure frozen in time.

"It's really you." Joseph cringed inwardly as he stood up. Why did his mouth always betray his thoughts?

Frederick chuckled and the skin around his eyes crinkled. "Indeed! Here I am in the flesh. I've barely slept since hearing about Nellie. But if there's one person who can wrestle an entire ocean and live to survive the tale, it's your mother."

"We know." Joseph studied Frederick's face, looking for a telltale sign of evil, but all he saw was an old man. Could he really have sabotaged Mum's boat when he was standing here telling them how upset he felt about her disappearance? Yet all of the evidence Flo and Joseph had already uncovered suggested so. Joseph suppressed a shiver. How could someone lie so well?

"We're grateful you got in touch," Flo added.

"I can only imagine how difficult it is for you." Frederick wrung his hands. "Especially with your father being away. I want to help bring Nellie and her crew home and I believe I have a plan for doing so. We'll discuss the details over dinner. Please, allow me to show you to the dining room."

"Is there time for a tour before dinner?" Flo asked.

"Yes," Joseph quickly added. "We've told Funmi and Isaac all about the wonders of Titan Towers, but I think they'd like to experience it for themselves." He marvelled at how easily the lie came out of his mouth.

From the smug look on Frederick's face, it seemed he'd swallowed their lies all too easily. "Of course! We'll pass by the kitchen and tell Cook to hold off on dinner." His eyes sparkled. "I'd be delighted to show you around. Much has changed since you were last here, Florence and Joseph. This way, children. Follow me!"

Frederick clapped his hands and led them out of the reception room and down the main corridor. Despite his older appearance, he moved fast. Dozens of warship paintings hung from the sleek, white walls.

"Titan Towers was built over forty years ago," Frederick said. "I used to look up at this hill as a young boy. It was my dream to build my home here and when my presenter career took off, I started work on this place." He opened a tall oak door. "Here's my office, where I used to plan all of The Titan's expeditions. Nowadays it's where I hold meetings for my various charitable endeavours."

The office was a long rectangular room with a large wooden desk facing the windows. There was a computer and phone on the desk, but no other documents or folders. It was tidy – almost too tidy for a room that Frederick supposedly used every day. The office looked like a movie set, everything perfectly staged, apart from the security cameras in every corner of the room with their green lights flashing ominously.

There was a single glass cabinet of awards next to the door and Joseph peered at the award engravings: *The Seabody Personal Award, Champion of the Earth Prize, Lifetime Achievement.* All of these accomplishments were fake and meaningless. Frederick didn't deserve any of it.

Joseph caught Isaac's eye and knew his best friend had had the same thought.

"There are quite a few levels in the house and I'd say, if we walk quickly enough, you can see them all!" Frederick chuckled. "Up to it?"

"Of course," Funmi replied, angelically. "I wouldn't want to miss anything."

"Jolly good." Frederick ushered them back towards the hallway. "Let's go."

The basement contained a vast wine cellar and a games room. The rest of the ground floor was taken up by the kitchen (the Cook was *not* happy about delaying dinner and Joseph almost got hit by a flying spatula), formal dining areas, informal living rooms and a security room.

"I've had a lot of attempted break-ins over the years, as you can imagine." Frederick opened the door to a guard sitting behind a desk with control panels and TV screens. "So I fully upgraded a couple of years ago."

Joseph saw Funmi lingering, trying to commit the security set-up to memory. It looked complicated and his hope of being able to sneak up to the turret started to dwindle.

Next up, the first floor contained ten bedrooms all with their own en-suite bathrooms. The bathtubs all looked bigger than the swimming pool at school. "I don't have many guests stay, but it's nice to have the space." Frederick shrugged. "I prefer my privacy now, after a life in the spotlight."

Of course you do, Joseph thought. When Frederick's back was turned, he looked at Flo. Her eyebrows had almost shot off her face.

The second floor was Joseph's favourite and he had to pinch himself on several occasions to pay attention to where the security cameras were, instead of gazing at the rows of bookshelves in the library and the gigantic screen in Frederick's home cinema.

"And that's the grand tour," Frederick said. They stood on the second-floor landing, waiting for the lift to take them back down. "I hope you liked it. My home is a reflection of my mighty accomplishments. I'm rather proud of it."

"It's incredible," Funmi fibbed. "Thank you for showing us."

But Joseph knew that Frederick hadn't shown them everything. He nudged Isaac, discreetly pointing to the end of the landing where the beginning of a stone staircase peeked out from behind a velvet curtain.

"What's over there?" Isaac asked in his best innocent voice. "Is there another level?"

"Oh that just leads to the turret. Nothing much up there apart from old junk. It's a bit of a dumping ground. Not worth showing you." Frederick cleared his throat just as the elevator arrived. "Now, let us eat. A feast awaits!" He ushered them through the doors and stood in front of them, blocking the view of the end of the corridor.

The entrance to the turret was clearly off limits and a place that Frederick didn't want to linger on for too long.

Joseph knew that made it the perfect place to hide secrets.

Chapter 15

A DECEITFUL DINNER

Over an extravagant dinner, Frederick Titan spoke about his equally extravagant rescue plan for Mum. Flo moved the seafood around her plate, trying to pretend she was eating as she listened. The four friends were all vegetarian; growing up right next to the sea and close to nature had had its effect.

"Ocean investigations are always tricky, but I have more boats and helicopters at my disposal than the Brinemouth police." Frederick bit the head off a king prawn before swallowing the rest. "That's why tomorrow morning, my team will set off to *The Ariel*'s last known location and conduct their own search and rescue mission. Linas will head up the team. He's a remarkable investigator. I'm awfully sorry they can't leave any sooner, but there are a few things we need to get in place."

"Thank you so much." It was the most difficult thank you of Flo's life. Not just because she didn't mean it, but because she feared what Frederick actually meant. He was pretending to help them, when all the evidence pointed towards him being responsible for Mum's disappearance. Was what he had just said a blatant lie or was he actually sending more of his people after Mum to take no chances?

"Do you know much about the North Atlantis? Or why Mum's boat might've gone missing in that specific part of the ocean?"

Flo gripped her spoon so hard the engravings on the handle left an imprint on her hand. What had happened to being subtle? Joseph had just asked the question equivalent of slapping someone in the face.

"I've travelled across the North Atlantis Ocean many times before." Frederick's bottom lip twitched slightly. "It can be treacherous and, as you know, Percy, God rest his soul, met his end there too. But your mother would've planned her route carefully. She was smarter than that."

"Our mum *is* smarter than that," Joseph replied.

"Quite." Frederick rubbed his chin. "Apologies."

The dining-room doors opened and a server holding a large platter of cakes and sweet treats appeared. Flo's stomach grumbled as a bowl of sticky toffee pudding was placed beside her.

"Please, dig in!" Frederick waved his fork in her direction. "You've barely touched a thing, the lot of you. I suppose kids these days do run on sugar."

Flo reached for her fork. As she nibbled on the sweet pudding and listened to Frederick talk all about the state-of-the-art vessel that would be used in the search for Mum, she couldn't help but notice how good he was at avoiding questions he didn't want to answer.

Scooping the last bit of toffee sauce from her dessert plate, Flo leaned back in her chair. Her stomach was full and her eyelids flickered. Thankfully, a kick under the table jolted her awake.

"Don't fall asleep," Joseph whispered.

Flo reached for her flute of sparkling apple juice. It was crisp and cold and revived her. She checked the grand clock hanging on the wall. It was twenty to eight. They had to meet Marianne back at the beach hut at ten-thirty with the island coordinates. Considering the hour-long journey through the Fortunia tunnel to reach the beach hut, there was no time to waste. They needed to sneak up to the turret now!

The doors opened again, but this time it was Linas who hurried over to Frederick. He bent down and whispered something in his ear. Flo wished she could hear their conversation.

Frederick nodded and Linas walked out of the room without saying a word. "Please excuse me, children." Frederick wiped his mouth with a napkin and scraped back his chair. "I have an important call to take in my office. I shouldn't be too long."

"Do you mind if I visit the library again?" Joseph spoke in his best scholarly voice. "You have so many incredible marine biology books."

"And you must have lots of film-making guides and manuals." Flo pointed to the camera round her neck. "Mum always said you were the reason she got into films and she's the reason why I want to be a film-maker too."

It was only a glimmer of hesitation, but Flo caught it on Frederick's face before he returned to his normal smile. "I don't see why not. Young creative minds should always be nourished! Do you remember the way?"

"We do," Flo said. "Such an incredible house sticks in the mind."

"Very well. I should only be twenty minutes or so. Meet me back down here when we're done and Linas will drive you home."

"Thank you again." Flo stood and stuck out her hand. This time, Frederick returned the gesture. She held his gaze, but this time his face gave nothing away.

"Anything for a friend. But please, Florence. No filming in Titan Towers." He looked down at her camera. "I'm a private person. Not everybody is as lucky as you to take a peek inside."

"I promise," Flo replied. She hoped crossing her fingers in her mind still counted.

Satisfied, Frederick nodded and left the room.

Flo pressed her ear to the dining-room door and waited until she heard the office door slam shut. She waited ten more seconds before signalling to the others.

"Let's go!"

They walked back down the hallway to where the stairs and elevator were located. Flo had just pressed the elevator button when Funmi spoke.

"For this to work, we need to turn off the security cameras," she said. "Didn't you see how many there were when he gave us the tour? Look how many there are in just this hallway!"

Flo slowly lifted her head. She counted at least ten tiny camera lenses fixed on different corners of the room. Funmi was right. They wouldn't get up to the turret without being spotted. "We need to turn those cameras off."

"You and Joseph go ahead," Funmi said. "Me and Isaac will head to the security room and handle it."

"But I have zero tech skills," Isaac said, alarmed.

"I don't need help with that, but I will need a distraction to get the guard out of the room. You'll need to keep him busy while I figure out the system."

"Right. Okay," Isaac looked much calmer. "I can do that." He removed the key card from his pocket and subtly passed it to Joseph. "Take this for the turret."

"I'll disable the cameras by the time you get to the second floor," Funmi continued. "You'll know when the green lights turn off. Then you can sneak up the turret staircase. But you'll need to be quick. I don't know how long it'll be until someone notices they're offline."

"How will you disable them?" Flo asked.

"Let me worry about that."

The glass elevator pinged open and before Flo could

say anything else, Funmi had pushed her and Joseph through the doors. They closed swiftly and, as they ascended, Flo saw Funmi and Isaac creeping back down the hallway.

"Alright then," Joseph said, taking a deep breath. "We're really doing this."

"We are." As the elevator took them higher, Flo looked out through its glass walls. She saw the sprawling garden of Titan Towers outside, full of exotic plants, marble sculptures and a large aviary. Wealth spilled from every corner of the place and now she knew the real reason behind Frederick's riches, Flo wanted to tear it all down with her bare hands.

The elevator announced its arrival. The doors jutted open and Flo stepped onto the landing, Joseph close behind her. The cinema and library doors were directly opposite them, with the hidden stone staircase at the end. She looked up at the security cameras, their green lights still flashing.

"They're still on," Joseph whispered. "Do you think something happened to the others?"

"C'mon, Funmi," Flo muttered under her breath. She crossed her fingers behind her back. She watched. She waited.

It started slowly, like a changing traffic light. The green flickered and then every camera on the landing turned red.

"She did it!" Joseph yelped. "They did it!"

There was no time to celebrate. Flo grabbed Joseph's hand and sprinted to the end of the hallway. She parted the curtain and they climbed the spiralling stone staircase two steps at a time, until, 255 steps later, there it was: the locked door in the turret staring back at them like a challenge.

Chapter 16

THE TRUTH IN THE TURRET

Joseph wasn't good at sneaking. The problem was that he had a permanently guilty face. Flo always teased him that he wouldn't last one minute during a police interrogation. As he stood on the turret staircase, jumping at every creak and echo, he hoped he'd never have to test that theory.

"Jojo, the key card!"

He passed it to Flo and with a single swipe against the sensor, the door clicked open.

The office they stepped into was nothing like the one downstairs. It was full of *things* and circular, with porthole windows that looked out onto a tiny balcony. The grand mahogany desk in the middle of the room was littered with documents, but a laptop peeked out from under the papers.

"Jackpot!" Flo tucked her hair behind her ears. "The island coordinates have got to be in here somewhere."

"The office downstairs must be for show," Joseph replied, following his sister over to the desk. "A double office to match his double life."

While Flo flicked through the documents, Joseph opened the laptop. The log-in screen appeared with the empty password box – the first obstacle to overcome. Once upon a time he would have considered himself an expert on Sir Frederick Titan, but now Joseph's former hero felt like a stranger.

"What would his password be?"

"It's got to be something about himself," Flo replied. "Try TITAN1234."

Joseph hesitated. "Surely he wouldn't use a common number sequence?"

"Do you have a better idea right now?"

Joseph didn't. He typed it in and pressed enter.

Incorrect password. Two attempts remaining.

"Nope." Joseph's nerves rattled inside him. "We've got two guesses left."

Flo groaned. "We need to get inside his laptop. All of

these documents are just bank statements. Nothing looks like a clue."

"What about something to do with Brinemouth?" Joseph offered. "His unofficial nickname in the city has always been *God.*"

"That's a good one. Try it!"

Joseph typed *GodofBrinemouth*

Incorrect password. One attempt remaining before system lock.

The fear set in. They had one more chance. Joseph racked his brain, thinking of every TV show, interview and book that he'd ever read about the great Frederick Titan.

"Hang on." He pictured The Titans poster on his bedroom wall, the team's motto printed in large letters. "Deeds Not Words was The Titans' motto. Frederick was the one who came up with it. But it had to be in Latin, obviously. Will that work?"

Flo shrugged. "Do it," she said.

Joseph carefully typed each letter, his heart thumping as he double-checked the spelling.

ActaNonVerba

He wished himself luck and pressed enter.

Instead of the error message, the log-in screen loaded.

"We're in!" Joseph's hands tingled with anticipation.

"Yes!" Flo slapped him on the back. "Good work, Jojo."

Joseph pulled up the search bar as the grandfather clock in the corner of the office ticked away. The security cameras had already been offline for five minutes and there was no way of knowing how much time was left. He typed the one word he was sure of. *Island*. It took a moment for the search to complete and then there it was, the only result: a folder on Frederick Titan's private network called FANTOME ISLAND. Joseph couldn't click on it quickly enough.

"This must be it!" Joseph's eyes darted between the two documents in the folder. *Fantome Island location map* and *Project W blueprint.* "This is the island that Mum was looking for!"

Flo grabbed her camera and pointed it at the laptop screen. "Open each file and I'll take as many pictures as I can."

Joseph pulled up both documents and Flo started snapping away. The *Location map* showed a circular-shaped island at the highest point of the North Atlantis Ocean. Numbers had been written just next to the island.

"The coordinates are there." Joseph pointed. "The longitude and latitude of the island. Zoom in."

"Yes, boss," Flo replied, teasingly. "I do know what coordinates are. You're not the only one who listens in geography lessons."

Joseph smiled. He was so used to feeling unsure that this new determination topped up his courage. He was Joseph Wanderday, stalwart sneaker and expert evidence finder!

"I'm not sure what this blueprint is supposed to be. Project W. What are you?" Flo muttered.

Glancing at the screen, Joseph tried to make sense of the random shapes and squiggly lines that ran across the blueprint. "If it's in the same folder, it must be important. We have to figure it out."

"And we will –" Flo let her camera fall against her chest after she'd snapped as many images as she could – "but there's not enough time to look through everything in detail right now. We can do that later with Marianne. I've taken hundreds of photos and a backup recording of the laptop screen. I think we've got everything we need."

The clock chimed eight.

"Let's get out of here." Joseph exited the folder and

logged out of the laptop, pushing it back under the messy documents. He double-checked that everything in the office looked just like they had found it. They couldn't be careless.

He looked at Flo standing by the open door, her eyes sparkling with accomplishment.

They had got what they had come for.

Now they needed to get as far away from Titan Towers as possible.

Chapter 17

A DOUBLE DEBRIEF

Flo fell through the elevator doors as they opened onto the ground floor, her feet moving as quickly as her mind as she ran towards Funmi and Isaac. They looked unscathed, thankfully, and were sitting on a bench in the hallway.

"You guys!" she panted. "You're never going to guess what Jojo found."

"And what may that be, pray tell?"

Frederick's voice pierced through Flo like a fishing spear. She turned round to see him standing at the bottom of the stairs. Where had he come from?

"Erm…" Being at a loss for words was a first for Flo. Frederick's hard stare took the breath from her lungs.

Her already warm cheeks reddened.

"I found a first edition of Dr Moray's *Marine Multiverse* in your library," Joseph stepped in. "I had to show it to Flo!"

"Yes." She followed her brother's lie. "He's Jojo's hero!"

"I thought I was?" Frederick curled his top lip.

"You are!" Joseph blushed. "Of course you are."

"I'm only teasing, boy." Frederick's mouth split into a menacing smile. "Did you know it's one of only fifty copies? I paid a lot of money for that book."

Flo's shoulders untensed, but she placed a protective hand round her camera. The need to find out more about Fantome Island was like a hunger. She glanced over at Joseph, hovering by the entrance, and knew he wanted to get far away from Titan Towers.

"I'm glad you all enjoyed looking around the library," Frederick said. "My call was cut short as there was a slight security issue."

"Oh no!" Flo tried to keep a straight face; she didn't dare look at Funmi. "Is everything okay?"

"My dear security guard, Jeffrey, somehow managed to lock himself outside in the courtyard without his key card," Frederick bristled. "The system went down, but we're back up and running."

Maybe it was the guilt she felt, but Flo could've sworn that Frederick sounded somewhat accusatory. She went to speak, but Joseph's huge yawn cut through the hallway. "Thank you for your hospitality," he said. "But I think we should be getting back home. Today has been exhausting."

"He's right," Flo added. "Dad is coming home early tomorrow morning, so we need to rest. Thank you for everything you're doing for Mum."

"You are most welcome." Frederick half-bowed. "I will keep your father updated about my search-and-rescue mission. Linas is bringing round the car as we speak to take you home."

Flo gave Funmi a look that communicated the plan; the type of look only a best friend can decipher. Funmi got to her feet and looped her arm through Isaac's. "Thank you for letting us inside your incredible home."

"Goodnight, Sir Titan." Flo made for the door. One foot in front of the other until she made it back to the safety of the Fortunia. Home.

"Wait a moment."

Flo froze.

"Have you received any other offers of help?" Frederick's voice had a hardened edge. "Aside from the police. I understand that there were a whole host of journalists outside the Fortunia this morning."

Flo turned round. "Yes, there were, but no one else has offered to help."

"So no one's been in contact with you?" Frederick stepped closer and she smelled the sickly sweetness of dessert on his breath. "No one from your mother's past?"

Flo remembered what Marianne had said, how she was being followed by Frederick's spies. Did he already know that Marianne had made contact with them? Or was he simply fishing? Flo could dance around the question or, as a boldness struck her, she could fish for information of her own.

"No one apart from yourself and the other Fortunia residents," she said. "Why? Is there someone else who could help?"

Frederick shook his head. "I'm just a curious old man." His smile was less friendly than it had been at the beginning of the evening. "I'm the only one in Brinemouth with the resources to bring Nellie home. But there will be people who say things about me. Untrue things, born of jealousy. Just remember that I am on your side. Always."

"We know."

The sound of Joseph's voice almost broke Flo. To anyone else, he might have sounded confident. But she knew her brother better than anyone. It had taken great strength for him to lie right back to Frederick's face. He'd been one of Joseph's heroes for so long. But, after today, the world had shifted on its axis. Nothing would ever be the same again.

The journey home was deathly quiet. As Linas drove down the hill and back towards the city, Flo looked at Joseph. His eyes flickered to the driver screen, as though worried that Linas had X-ray vision. She gave him a reassuring smile before turning back to the window as home came into view.

Nobody spoke when Linas dropped them outside the Fortunia other than a whispered *Thank you*. Nobody spoke as they walked across the lobby and called the elevator. As soon as Flo closed the door to their apartment, everyone burst into life.

"We found the island!" Joseph squealed. "We've got the coordinates. And a blueprint! Project W. We haven't worked out what that is yet, but we will. Anyway, I guessed his password and we broke into his personal computer. Flo took photos and recordings because it wasn't like we could print it all off from his laptop. But we've got it. We got it!"

Isaac high-fived a breathless Joseph.

"Coming up for air anytime soon, Jojo?" Flo laughed at the excitement on her brother's face. "We couldn't have done it without you two, though. How did you disable the cameras?"

"The security system was the same one we have at the adventure park." Funmi brushed her shoulder. "There's a hidden switch underneath the control panel that temporarily disables the cameras."

"My distraction worked perfectly," Isaac added. "I used the leftover sticky toffee pudding we had for dessert to cover up the main courtyard camera. When the guard went to see why it wasn't working, I locked him outside."

Flo laughed again. The image of Isaac running around Titan Towers with sticky cake hands was fully believable.

"Good gills, I don't ever want to go back to that place! It gave me the creeps." Funmi leaned against the hallway cabinet. "Just like Frederick, actually. And what he said about sending a search-and-rescue boat to look for your mum. What do you think he meant by that?"

"It could be a straight-up lie," Flo said.

"Or maybe," Joseph stuttered, "maybe Mum and her crew reached the island and Frederick's sending Linas there."

Flo sensed a "what if" on the tip of her brother's tongue. It was the same one in her head too: *What if Mum is trapped on Fantome Island?*

"In that case, we better get a move on." Flo clapped her hands. "Last chance to stay in Brinemouth, you two."

Funmi and Isaac shook their heads so hard Flo thought they might fly off.

"No chance." Isaac crossed his arms. "We've already come this far together."

"FSquared always," Funmi said. "Where you go, I go."

Flo noticed Joseph's smile and knew what he was thinking. There wasn't much that the four friends wouldn't do for each other. They were family.

"Go and pack a bag for the journey," Flo instructed, "and meet in the basement kitchen ASAP."

Funmi saluted. "I'll tell my folks I'm staying at your place for a sleepover."

"I'll say the same," Isaac said, before pulling a face. "Unless my dad isn't at home, which he probably won't be if he's still trying to fix the Fortunia's rubbish chute."

He waved glumly and followed Funmi out of the apartment. Joseph sprinted to his room and Flo heard his grunts and objects flying through the air.

Flo raced round the apartment. She grabbed the medical kit from under the bathroom sink and raided the kitchen cupboards for breakfast bars and crisps. She pocketed a couple of kelp gobstoppers; Flo had to have Mum's favourite sweets for when they found her. In Flo's bedroom, she stuffed her clothes, spare camera batteries and Zelda, her toy octopus, into her rucksack. Zelda had been her comfort blanket ever since she was small and would be until she was old and grey.

Five minutes later, Flo was back in the hallway. Joseph was standing by the already ajar door, his green rucksack almost as big as his body.

"You ready?"

"As ready as I'll ever be." Joseph fiddled with his rucksack straps. "I'll go and call the elevator."

Before she closed the door behind her, Flo took one last look at her home. She gazed up at the family portrait that hung above Mum's awards cabinet and breathed in the smell of lemon salt that forever lingered in the hallway – Dad's own concoction to stop the apartment from constantly smelling of paint fumes.

Now she thought of Dad and how in less than ten hours he'd walk through the door and find that she and Joseph were gone. Guilt nagged at her, despite her attempts to squash it down. She reminded herself that Dad would never let them travel across the ocean alone.

Flo had to concentrate on the journey ahead, so that the next time she walked through the door, Mum would be walking right beside her.

And they'd all be home. Together again.

Chapter 18

ESCAPE FROM BRINEMOUTH

"You kids have outdone yourselves."

Joseph blushed, thankful it was dark inside Marianne's cramped beach hut.

"Seriously," Marianne continued, "you broke into Frederick's secret office *and* hacked his laptop to find the island coordinates and the project blueprint." She gave Joseph an encouraging smile. "Never doubt yourself. You kids are capable of anything. Flo, zoom in on the map again."

Joseph had only quickly glanced at the map earlier that night, but now his eyes took in every detail as Flo held the camera still and flicked through the photos of the map. The island was circular and a sprawling forest seemed to cover most of its land. In the middle was a volcano, surrounded by a lake.

"The volcano is on its own island in the middle of that lake," Isaac said. "Do you think it's still, like, active?"

A shrug had never been less reassuring. "Volcanoes are a beast of their own," Marianne said. "It could be active, dormant or extinct."

"Right." Joseph's eyes widened in alarm, picturing fire and spewing molten lava. East of the lake was a small grid of cabins, but it was something else that grabbed his attention. Joseph had almost missed it before, but there was a rectangular building at the foot of the volcano with a scribbled description beneath it.

"A laboratory?" He looked at Marianne. "Did you and Mum know there was a laboratory on the island?"

Marianne shook her head.

But there was no elation in the beach hut for this breakthrough; it brought only a new type of fear.

"What does Frederick need a laboratory for?" Isaac asked.

"Experiments, I'd guess," Flo said.

Joseph pictured a cold, clinical lab. Scientists in white coats and goggles. The sharp edge of a scalpel.

Microscopes and test tubes. "You said Linas was trying to recruit another scientist to work for Frederick. They must be working on something inside the laboratory. Maybe that's what Project W is."

Marianne nodded and reached for her satchel. "Let's get out of here. We'll look through the blueprint properly once we've set sail."

Under cover of darkness they left the beach hut behind. Despite the late hour, it was still warm outside and the air was as thick as chowder. Marianne led them down the rickety porch stairs and across the beach front – a wide empty expanse of sand and smoothed pebbles. The safety of the beach hut was gone and Joseph found himself glancing over his shoulder.

"The main port entrance is only a ten-minute walk from here," Marianne said. "I found a vessel we can borrow."

Joseph frowned. "Borrow?"

"We'll return it before the owner even realizes it's gone," Marianne replied, nonchalant.

Joseph thought better than to protest; he'd stolen plenty from Titan Towers earlier. It was all for a worthwhile reason, he told himself.

"The guards at the port are easy to sneak past, but I

can't be certain I've entirely shaken off Frederick's spies," Marianne said.

"How long have they been following you?" Joseph doubled his pace to keep up with Marianne.

"Ever since I returned to Brinemouth, three years ago, to investigate with your mum. This city is my home too, but Frederick's people would approach me in public. Tell me I should leave, if I knew what was good for me. And not to make any trouble. I knew he was behind it." Marianne's nose crinkled like a bad smell. "When the threats got worse, I tried to lay low. Wore disguises."

"That doesn't sound like a fun way to live," Joseph said.

"It isn't. I've sacrificed a lot for the sake of my work and chasing after a good story. But investigating Frederick Titan has been the most dangerous yet. I'll never be able to live a normal life until we stop him."

The sadness in her voice startled Joseph. His mind flitted through possible responses, but none of them seemed good enough. All that did was a simple, "I'm sorry."

"Don't be. That will all change once we find your mum." Marianne cleared her throat. "We'll take him down and we'll all be free."

Flo brushed past Joseph with impatient strides. "How are we getting into the port? I guess we can't exactly walk through the main entrance."

"There's a hole in one side of the fence," Marianne explained. "Stick close to me and follow my movements. I know the port layout inside out."

Sand soon turned to concrete under their feet as they reached the path that led along the sea wall. Seaport was eerily quiet. The old industrial neighbourhood had always unsettled Joseph. There were no amusement arcades, cafes or shops, just the run-down buildings and piles of waste littering the border between land and sea. Lost in his thoughts, he bumped into the back of Marianne. She'd come to a stop behind an empty cargo container.

"We're here," she said. "The fence is just ahead of us."

Joseph copied Marianne's movements and poked his head round the container. He saw the towering metal fence that surrounded the port's perimeter. A bright light shone from a watchtower, moving back and forth like a pendulum.

"We're going to have to run, aren't we?" Isaac asked.

Marianne nodded. "If the light comes towards you, get as low as you can. Stay down until it's gone."

Fear made every single part of Joseph's body tense. What if he tripped? He checked his shoelaces were tied and watched the light move in the opposite direction.

"Let's go!"

Joseph sprinted after Marianne. The light was somewhere behind them, but he concentrated on putting one foot in front of the other. His chest tightened, lungs puffing, as he ran across the empty land. There was no cover here. All it would take was one guard looking his way and it was over.

The broken-down area of fence came into view and Joseph stretched out his arms, ready to pull himself through the hole. Marianne went first, jumping feline-like. He shrugged off his rucksack and passed it to her before following. He twisted his left leg through and found his balance before lifting his right leg, making himself small and pulling his whole body through the hole. He was inside!

"Catch this!" Isaac threw his bag through. It hit Joseph square in the face.

Isaac winced as he emerged from the hole. "Sorry."

"It's fine." Joseph rubbed his face. "Where are the—?"

Horror clamped his throat shut when he saw the

watchtower light sweeping towards Flo and Funmi. It was moving fast, creeping closer and they threw themselves to the ground. Joseph turned cold. If they were spotted now it would be over. The light had reached the top of Flo's head when a loud alarm blared from somewhere inside the port. Then came the sound of metal smashing and the gruff, angry shouts of the guards. The light retreated, following a new direction towards the other side of the port.

"Come on!" Joseph found his voice again. "It's clear!"

Flo and Funmi jumped to their feet and sprinted to the fence. Joseph and Isaac helped pull them through until they were all safely inside the port.

"What was that noise?" Funmi took a deep swig from her water bottle and splashed a few drops on her face.

Marianne shrugged. "Maybe we're not the only ones going somewhere we shouldn't tonight."

"You alright?" Joseph spotted a cut on Flo's cheek.

"It's nothing. Just a graze." She roused a smile. "I've survived worse."

The route through the port was like playing a real-life game of Tetris. They navigated a maze of cargo containers, turning back when met with dead ends and the sound of a patrolling guard. Marianne had said she knew the way, but Joseph felt like they were going in circles.

"Are you sure you know where you're going?"

"We're close by," Marianne said.

Flo nudged Joseph. "Marianne knows her stuff. We have to trust her."

"I—" Joseph opened his mouth to argue back, but he knew Flo was right. The journey to find Mum would only be successful if they all trusted each other. They were a team now and had to work together.

Rounding the last stack of containers minutes later, Joseph saw his first glimpse of the water. Six boats were moored next to a wooden dock.

"Which one's ours?" he asked.

Marianne pointed to the end of the dock, beyond the boats.

"There's nothing there?" Joseph's frustration spiked.

"Look in the water," Marianne replied.

At the end of the dock was a submarine, its top half gently bobbing above the water.

"Wow!" Joseph rushed past the others, desperate for a closer look. The submarine was a cylinder shape with the top of three oval windows peeking out of the water. A long, thin radio antenna stuck out of the top next to a square hatch. Joseph gasped. Even with the rest of it hidden underwater, he would've recognized *The Earle* anywhere.

It was Dr Moray's submarine.

Chapter 19

ALL ABOARD THE EARLE

"We're travelling on a submarine?" Joseph heard the surprise in his sister's voice.

"This isn't any old submarine." He turned round, trying to get his words out as he pointed enthusiastically. "This is *The Earle*! It belongs to Dr Moray!"

Isaac's eyes bulged like a colossal squid. "Woah, wait up. This is his research sub?"

Joseph nodded and returned his best friend's excited smile before a worry set in.

"You borrowed Dr Moray's submarine?" He looked at Marianne. "There's no way of him linking it back to us, is there?"

Marianne shrugged and climbed the narrow ladder

steps on the side of the submarine up to the hatch. Next to the square metal hatch was the security keypad. "I don't think so. I don't know for sure, but I doubt it."

Joseph didn't feel reassured.

Marianne pressed various buttons on the keypad, mumbling numbers under her breath. There was a long beep followed by a hiss and then the top of the hatch opened.

One by one they shrugged off their rucksacks and lowered themselves through the hatch. Fascination won over Joseph's worry as he walked down the narrow entranceway and into the main living quarters. On the left were two sets of bunk beds and a fold-out table and bench. In the middle of the room the galley was boxed in by cupboards with just enough room for a small stove and a countertop. And on the right was a metallic door leading to the control room. The door was ajar and Joseph spotted Marianne flicking buttons on a large panel. Isaac stood next to her watching the panel light up like festive decorations.

"Can someone secure the hatch?" Marianne called.

"On it!" Flo and Funmi replied.

"Make sure the light directly underneath the hatch turns red," Marianne added. She started up the engine and slowly steered them away from the dock. "That will mean it's fully watertight."

Joseph joined Isaac and Marianne in the control room. He'd always dreamed of seeing the wonders of the ocean up close. This wasn't how he'd imagined it happening, though. "Do you know how to pilot this thing?" he asked.

"I worked on a sub a few years back with an ocean conservation group." Marianne brushed her hair back from her face. "Got piloting lessons in exchange for writing articles about the work they were doing."

"Hatch is secure," Funmi called.

"Perfect. We'll start to pull away from the dock." Marianne nodded at the two steering wheels. "I can control the stern rudder and horizontal fins, but I need someone to move the horizontal planes. They're at the back of the sub and help it to submerge and ascend."

"You're asking me to help?" Joseph's voice turned squeaky.

"Your mum taught you a thing or two about boats, didn't she?"

Joseph thought of the summer days he'd spent with Mum on *The Ariel*. "But I don't know anything about submarines. I—"

"Go on, mate." Isaac nudged him. "You got this."

Joseph positioned himself behind the second steering wheel. His hands gripped the cold metal and his panic doubled.

"Just relax and pull the wheel slowly to your chest," Marianne encouraged. "I'm right here with you."

Joseph followed her instruction and gently pulled the wheel towards him. It was lighter than he expected.

"Excellent," Marianne said. "You're doing great."

Behind him, Joseph heard the door open.

"Why are we still floating?" Funmi asked.

"We won't for much longer," Marianne replied. "We're going down slowly, but the main ballast tank needs to fill with water."

"Come again?"

"You vent out the air and replace it with water, which means that the density of the sub is greater than the water," Joseph explained, not taking his eyes off the wheel. "It's called negative buoyancy."

"Science rules," Isaac confirmed.

"So we'll get heavier and sink?" Flo sounded interested, which surprised Joseph. Science wasn't his sister's favourite subject.

Marianne nodded. "We'll sink in a controlled way.

Once we get to our destination we'll need to drain the water and pump compressed air into the tank. That will help us surface again."

"Roger, Captain!" Isaac grinned. "Shall we go and unpack while you get us underwater – I mean underway?"

"Please, no terrible jokes," Funmi groaned. "There's nowhere to hide from them in here."

While the others settled in the living quarters, Joseph stayed at Marianne's side, gently pulling the wheel closer at her command. The water rose around them as they moved away from the dock. They were about to enter the underwater world, a place he'd learned about from Dr Moray's books and Mum's stories. Now he was experiencing it for himself and Joseph held on to that thought. When they were reunited with Mum he'd tell her their own story of how they'd found their way across the ocean to bring her home.

The top of the submarine was almost surface level with the water when Joseph spotted a figure on the dock illuminated by the security lights. He blinked and, when his eyes focused, he almost let go of the wheel in fright.

"Linas!" Joseph panicked. "He's here!"

Blood rushed loudly through Joseph's ears as he watched Linas hold up a camera to his face. Then there was a bright flash, just like the one earlier in the square, and Joseph realized who'd been following his family all this time. Frederick hadn't sent just any of his spies to keep tabs on the Wanderdays, he'd sent his right-hand man.

"Don't worry." Marianne hit an overhead button and a high-pitched beep sounded. The screen lit up with a long, thin line. "The coordinates to Fantome Island are locked in."

A shadow fell over the submarine as it fully submerged and Linas disappeared from view. The interior lights flicked on and Joseph almost slumped forward from the relief.

But the relief was short-lived as a kaleidoscope of feelings and emotions spun inside him. Fear that Linas might follow them. Anxiety about what awaited them on this journey. Excitement that they'd taken control and were no longer sitting at home worrying. Sadness at leaving Dad behind and causing him more worry. And hope. Hope that they'd find Mum and her crew.

Joseph looked out of the window and saw nothing but murky blue and green.

They were underwater. There was no turning back now.

All that stood between Joseph and Mum was the rest of the ocean.

Recording #2:

JOURNEY TO FANTOME ISLAND

It's just gone five in the morning and everyone is sleeping in their bunk apart from Marianne and me. She's been navigating us through the waters, keeping watch for any sign of Mum's boat as well as any others that might be following us. We're still a day away from reaching the beginning of the North Atlantis Ocean.

I know I should rest, but sleep won't come. Instead, I'm sat by the middle window watching the world outside. I've seen shoals of vibrant mandarin fish, a leatherback turtle baring its spiky teeth and a couple of spinner dolphins. I want to wake Joseph so he can see them too, but he looks so peaceful sleeping. Spotting Linas on the dock really shook him up, but we have a good head start. Even if Frederick sends Linas after us now, on his fake rescue mission, time is on our side to put distance between us.

Being this close to the ocean is incredible but bittersweet. I wish Mum was here so I could tell her how I have the same magical feeling she's always described. Instead she's missing somewhere out there, whether that's in the water or on Fantome Island with the rest of her crew. All because she dared to take a stand against Frederick Titan.

I've been going over every photo and recording I took of the documents on Frederick's laptop, the map and the blueprint. I think the blueprint looks like a machine, but I can't figure out what it's supposed to be for. I'll ask Funmi when she wakes up – hopefully she can make more sense of it with her engineer's brain.

I've studied the map so many times my eyes have started to blur, but I want to commit every inch of Fantome Island to memory. The dense forests, the lake surrounding the volcano. The cabins that look like a small housing area. And the laboratory. I keep circling back to it. It feels like the reason why Frederick has kept the island's existence a secret. Whatever Project W is…it's something he wants to keep far away from prying eyes. With everything I now know about Frederick Titan's true self, I also know that this project cannot be good.

We have to find Mum first and then, together, we'll find out what's happening on Fantome Island.

I asked Marianne about the name of the island. She told me that phantom islands were islands that were once thought to have existed hundreds of years ago. These islands appeared on maps but, over time, explorers discovered that they didn't exist. It was a navigational mistake or simply make-believe, a place that someone had invented to trick and deceive.

It makes sense for Frederick to call it Fantome Island. He's tricked the world for a long time, pretending to be someone he isn't.

This journey and our film will carry on the work that Mum and Marianne started a long time ago.

We will pull back the curtain on Frederick Titan.

His time of tricking the world is almost up.

Chapter 20

THE GREAT UNKNOWNS

Joseph knew bad news was coming when Flo insisted that everyone ate breakfast before they discussed the map and blueprint. While she attacked a cereal bar, Joseph nervously nibbled on a tamarind ball. Funmi had brought the snack because they were her and Joseph's favourite, but his stomach felt too unsettled to enjoy them.

"We survived the night and didn't sink." Isaac sat down at the table and took a celebratory swig of orange juice. "Cheers to that!"

"Glad to see the bar for my piloting abilities was so low," Marianne replied from the control room.

"No!" Isaac spluttered. "I didn't mean it like that.

You're doing great."

"Relax, kid." Marianne laughed. "I'm joking."

The submarine passed a seamount and Joseph spotted dying whitewashed coral poking out of the underground mountain. His heart ached picturing the vibrant colours that the coral had been before the water had warmed and bleached the coral.

"Where are we now?" Flo asked.

"About a quarter of the way to Fantome Island's coordinates," Marianne replied. "We'll reach the start of the North Atlantis Ocean by nightfall. If we keep to the same speed we should arrive by tomorrow afternoon."

Another day! Joseph's whole body tensed. They had to find Mum quicker than that. He pictured Linas on the dock. If he was coming after them, how long would it take for him to catch up in one of Frederick's state-of-the-art boats?

"Jojo!" Flo waved her arm in front of his face. "Come back to us."

"Sorry." He blinked. "I'm listening."

"So I stayed up most of last night looking through the map and the blueprint from Frederick's laptop." Flo placed her camera in the middle of the table. "The

Project W blueprint looks like a type of machine, but I can't figure it out. I need your science-y and technical brains."

Joseph looked closely at the camera screen, his eyes taking in every detail of the blueprint. If it was a machine, it looked to be made up of a large empty aquarium tank with four individual compartments. Four long lines, possibly signifying wires, fed through a hole at the top and attached to a helmet in each compartment. A smaller, separate square sat at the base of the tank.

"It looks –" he tried to find the right word for how the machine made him feel – "scary."

"I've never seen anything like that before." Funmi nibbled the end of her braid. "Did you find any explanation for it? Technical documents? A user manual?"

"No, nothing," Flo replied. "Marianne helped me look through the rest of the photos I took, but there was nothing that explained the machine."

"The helmets suggest that something or someone can be attached," Isaac said.

"Someone? Like people?" Funmi shivered.

"Or any animal with a head," Joseph offered, creeping himself out simultaneously. "But what about the wires?"

"Wires normally transport electricity, or some other type of energy," Funmi said. "But from this blueprint it's not clear what the wires are attached to at the other end."

"The only way to know that for sure is to find it," Flo said. "The blueprint and the map were in the same Fantome Island folder on Frederick's laptop, so the machine must be on the island."

"We should start our search in the laboratory." The beginning of a plan was starting to form in Joseph's head. It was becoming real, something he could hold on to.

Flo nodded and flicked to the images of the island map. "But our first priority is finding Mum and her crew. If we haven't found any trace of *The Ariel* by the time we reach the island, I think we should focus our efforts on searching ashore."

Both possibilities filled Joseph with dread. Mum and her crew stranded somewhere in the ocean made him feel sick. Yet the thought of them on Frederick's island was worse now Joseph knew what the man was capable of.

"The island is mainly covered by the forest," Flo continued. "It's the heart of the island, where the volcano and lake are, that interests me most. There are two paths that lead there through the forest."

As Flo zoomed out, Joseph turned his attention to the cabins east of the volcano lake. "Do you think that's where the scientists live? The ones that Frederick recruited for the project."

"I thought the same," Isaac said. "Maybe they keep prisoners there too."

"Like maybe your mum and her crew," Funmi added.

"It's a possibility." Flo sounded as calm as a still pond; Joseph didn't understand how. "The laboratory and the cabins are the two places we should focus our search for Mum. There'll be a lot of ground to cover. So—"

His sister's pause stole Joseph's breath. He wasn't going to like whatever came next.

"I think we should split up."

There it was. "Split up?" Joseph repeated, astounded. "We can't!"

"Why not?" Flo frowned. "We split up at Titan Towers and that worked out just fine."

"This is different and you know it." Joseph spluttered out each word. "We're far from Brinemouth and way out of our comfort zone." He looked to Funmi and Isaac for backup. They both looked equally shocked.

"We've watched so many horror movies together, Flo," Funmi said, "so you know it's *never* a good idea to split up on a secret island!"

"And the funny sidekicks *always* die first," Isaac moaned.

"Hold your seahorses." Flo's voice cut through the noise. "This is the best way to search the entire island. If Mum and her crew are there we need to work fast. Linas is probably already on our tail. And if one of us gets captured, or injured, there'll be another team who can carry on. It's the best way. It's the only way."

Dread sat in Joseph's stomach at the thought of them being apart. There were too many unknowns, too many possibilities of what could go wrong.

"To be fair," Funmi said, her tone softening, "I suppose we've already taken about a million risks. And they've all paid off so far."

"Don't exaggerate," Isaac interrupted. "More like five."

"Whatever," Flo retorted. "The exact number doesn't matter. All that matters is finding Mum. If she's on the island, this is our best chance of doing that."

A loud beeping sound interrupted the conversation and Joseph almost knocked a plate from the table as he turned towards the control room. "What was that? Are we in trouble?"

"Stay calm," Marianne called. She'd been quiet until now, focused on piloting the submarine through increasingly choppy waters. "I'm handling it."

Joseph ran to Marianne's side, the others close behind him. The flashing red lights on the control panel made his stomach flip. Red meant danger. Pulsating, nerve-splitting danger.

"There's something nearby." Marianne pointed at the sonar display screen. It showed a glowing red circle that seemed to be inching closer to the blue E, which stood for *The Earle*, their submarine. Joseph felt like all the air from his lungs had been squeezed out.

"What is it?" Isaac asked.

"I'm not sure." Marianne tapped her cheeks. Her face scrunched up in concentration and, for the first time, she looked scared. "We'd better take precautions. If it's another sub, it'll have a sonar detector." She reached for the largest button and turned off the humming engine. "We need to silence everything inside *The Earle*. Right now."

Chapter 21

A SATSUMA GHOST

Everyone sprang into action. Funmi and Flo gathered the breakfast plates from the table and stacked them in the galley cupboards. Isaac turned off the radio and killed the lights. Joseph and Marianne switched off as many of the control panel functions as they could, apart from the ones that retained the submarine's buoyancy. They had to be silent, but they couldn't sink.

All now huddled around Marianne's pilot chair, Joseph looked out into the murky water. He reached for Flo's hand in the darkness. Neither of them said aloud what they feared the most, but they didn't need to. The fear that Linas had caught them took up all the space in Joseph's brain.

What actually appeared from the water was nothing he could have predicted. Two bright orange eyes emerged from behind a rock formation. It took a moment to realize that the eyes weren't just floating; they were attached to a transparent head.

"What is that?" Flo whispered.

Joseph shrugged. He'd never heard of this creature or read about it in any of Dr Moray's books. It had a mouth like a clown's smile and its large body followed, long and red, like a lobster. Its tail split into four long tentacles, reaching out like beckoning fingers.

As it came closer, the head flitted with sparks of blue and green light. The creature was bioluminescent. Had it swum up from the very bottom of the ocean floor? Joseph was used to feeling mixed emotions, but this combination of fear and absolute awe was new to him. Was this strange, beautiful creature about to swallow them whole? Its gaping mouth grew wider and larger and Joseph closed his eyes, waiting for one of the tentacles to grip the submarine. He wouldn't find Mum and he'd never see her again. Or Dad. He'd never get to Fantome Island and stop Frederick Titan. All of the things he would never get to do ran through his head as Joseph waited for darkness to engulf him.

But it didn't come.

Slowly, he opened his eyes to see the creature retreating into the murky depths. Joseph went to move, but Flo held him back until the creature and the red circle on the sonar screen fully disappeared from view.

"We're safe." Marianne slumped in her chair. "That was close."

"What *was* that thing?" Funmi flipped a switch and the interior of *The Earle* was bathed in light.

"Never seen anything like it." Marianne rubbed her forehead. "The ocean is an endless gift."

The engine of *The Earle* whirred back into life and Joseph returned to his bunk, his mind alive. He grabbed his notebook, stored safely under his pillow, and flicked to a blank page.

"That was incredible." Isaac sat down at the end of his bunk. "And terrifying."

"I was just going to log it." Joseph smiled, unsurprised his best friend had felt the same.

"We could be the first ones to have ever seen it." Isaac's hands danced through the air. "This could make us celebrities in the marine biology world!"

Joseph pulled two pencils from his rucksack. "Let's write down everything we can remember and be as detailed as possible. When we find Mum, we can show it to her too. Maybe she'll feature our finding at the Institute!"

Isaac nodded enthusiastically. He scribbled down a few notes and held up the page.

"What's a satsuma ghost?" Joseph asked, earnestly.

"You know," Isaac pointed to his face as though it was obvious. "The creature had orange eyes and a translucent head. I thought it deserved a unique name."

Laughter bubbled at Joseph's lips, but he swallowed it back down. Isaac looked so serious and genuine. "I don't think we'll be taken seriously by anyone if we say we saw a piece of haunted fruit lurking in the ocean."

"Fine, I'll think of something else." Isaac crossed out his scribbles. "But it was a catchy name. I stand by it."

Joseph gave his best friend an encouraging smile. It was catchy, but somehow, calling it a satsuma ghost downplayed just how scary the creature had been.

The ocean was full of magic, but it was also terrifying.

And what Joseph found most surprising was that he didn't mind it one bit.

Chapter 22

UNCHARTED TERRITORY

Flo wasn't used to feeling so on edge. The wonder of the underwater world had quickly turned to fear after their close encounter with the strange ocean creature, and she'd retreated to the safety of her top bunk. It dawned on her that this wasn't the type of adventure she'd read about in stories, where friends travelled to magical lands and defeated mythical creatures. No magic or myth awaited them. Only the unknown and actual fang-sharp danger.

"Hey, sis." Joseph's head appeared by the side of her bunk. He climbed the last few rungs and flopped onto her bed. "I was thinking about your plan and how we should split up."

Flo prepared herself for another protest, but Joseph reached into his pocket and pulled out a pair of portable radios.

"I found these in the storage cupboard. They have a two-way transceiver so we can use them to keep in touch with each other on the island."

"Do they work?" Flo asked, trying to hide her surprise.

"I'm not sure. They turn on, but all I get is static."

"Hey, Funmi," Flo called. "We need your brain!"

Funmi swivelled on her table seat. "What's up?"

"Can you take a look at these?" Flo pointed at the radios in Joseph's hands. "Jojo's getting static."

"The antennas have probably come loose." Funmi hurried over to grab the radios. "Nothing the daughter of an engineer can't fix." She emptied her rucksack onto the table and out fell a screwdriver and various other tools.

"Did you bring these from home?" Isaac asked as a wrench almost landed on his hand.

"Obviously." Funmi rolled her eyes at him. "You never know when you're going to need tools." She set to work carefully taking the radios apart so they could be put back together better.

"I don't want us to split up," Joseph said quietly, so only Flo could hear, "but I didn't want any of this to happen. If it's what we have to do to find Mum then we'll do it. We said we'd jump…"

"…right in and play with everything we've got," Flo finished the sentence.

Joseph climbed back down her bunk and she watched him sit by the window, a smile of wonder on his face and a notebook and pen in his hands. He seemed different down here, like the water eased the weight of his worries. Flo wished for Joseph to feel that way for ever.

The day dragged its heels as they journeyed across the ocean. Flo wished for magical powers to speed up time, but all she could do was wait. Waiting, she quickly discovered, was something you couldn't escape. By the time evening approached, Funmi was still working on the radios. Joseph and Isaac hadn't moved from the window all day, detailing their ocean life discoveries in their notebooks.

Flo grabbed her camera and climbed down from her bunk. She needed a distraction and she slipped into the control room to find Marianne sitting in the pilot seat, her face fixed in concentration.

"Mind if I do some filming?" Flo pointed the camera at Marianne, who held a hand against her face.

"Of course. Just not of me," she squirmed. "I'm not very photogenic."

"Sorry. I get that. I always prefer being behind a camera rather than in front of it."

Flo panned over to the window where bioluminescent fish lit up the dark water. Their bodies looked like a constellation and it reminded Flo of when Mum had shown her how to spot Ursa Minor and Major from the Fortunia's rooftop. A pang of homesickness shook her body and it didn't go unnoticed.

"You holding up okay?" Marianne asked.

Flo hit pause as a swordfish with a thin scar on its bill swam past the window. Marianne patted the space next to her and Flo squeezed onto the chair. The dam wall that she'd built in her brain, ever since the news report yesterday morning, slowly weakened.

"There's so many unknowns. I've always liked being in control and having a plan. I've been telling Jojo that we'll find Mum and her crew. But..." Flo bit her lip. "What if we don't?"

Marianne wrapped her arms round Flo and her tears

finally arrived in great, silent waves, her shoulders rising and falling. Each time she felt she'd reached the surface of her sadness it pulled her back down. Flo's sadness was a monster, a kraken that wouldn't release its grip on her.

When she had no tears left to cry, Marianne spoke.

"Life is just like the ocean deep. It's a mystery. Every time we think we've figured out what lies beneath, something unexpected breaks through the surface. The only thing we can do is to face each day head on. But that's much easier when we're surrounded by love. There's not much that isn't made better with love."

"You're wise." Flo wiped her face. "Thanks."

"Not wise." Marianne winked. "Just old."

Flo laughed. "When we get back, will you stay in Brinemouth? It would be nice to get to know you better."

"I'd love that," Marianne smiled. "You know, I've been focused on my work for so long. Trying to save our planet is all-consuming and I forgot to live my life at the same time. There's so much I've missed."

The air turned heavy. Flo wanted to fill the silence and ask Marianne what she meant, but the look on her face spoke only of regrets.

"It's never too late to start," Flo said instead. "When

we finally expose Frederick you can come and stay with us at the Fortunia. Maybe you can even work with Mum at the Institute! Then on weekends we can go to the adventure park and eat chips for dinner."

Marianne beamed. "There's nothing I'd love more than to eat my body weight in chips with you."

A low-pitched beep sounded from the control panel and the happy look on Marianne's face quickly disappeared. "Looks like there's a row of larger seamounts up ahead." She reached for the steering wheel. "I need to navigate us through this bit. It could get tricky."

Flo turned her camera back on as the underwater mountains came into view. Sea anemones, every colour of the rainbow, sprouted from the cracks. As they got closer, the submarine's light illuminating the water, Flo spotted a ball of fishing nets and thick rope tangled together. It stretched over a long coral reef.

"Ghost nets." Marianne clenched her jaw. "See how they're choking that coral? They break up the reef, exposing it to infection."

"How did they get there?" Flo zoomed in on chunks of coral crumbling away.

"Often carelessness. Fishermen lose their nets over

the side of their boats. Sometimes they dump them too."

Flo gripped her camera tighter. "Humans don't deserve the ocean."

A sad smile flickered across Marianne's face. "You sound just like your mum. She always says humans are the most idiotic species."

The submarine was gently veering away from the nets when a flicker of something familiar caught Flo's eye.

"Wait!" Her camera fell through her hands. It swung from her neck strap as she jolted forward. "I saw something." She pointed towards a crack at the bottom of the closest seamount. "Can you shine the light over there again?"

"What is it?" Marianne moved the light back across the water, but Flo couldn't answer. Her voice was stuck, just like the part wreckage of a boat she saw. A single red panel that had once been attached to the hull of a boat was sticking out of the seamount crack. On it were two words painted in green.

The Ariel.

A part of Mum's boat was broken and discarded in the depths of the ocean. Instinct took over and Flo rushed to lock the control-room door. Joseph couldn't see this. If he did, he'd fall apart.

"This doesn't have to mean what you think it means," Marianne said. "There's no other wreckage here to indicate the entire boat sank. I've been searching the water for signs of life, and will continue to do so, but I don't think Nellie is lost at sea. Fantome Island is still our best bet."

"I know." Flo took a deep breath, but it didn't do much to calm her racing heart. Thinking positively normally came easily to her, but she struggled to feel reassured by Marianne's words. She looked back out at the broken hull panel, flakes of its red paint floating away, and pictured one of Frederick Titan's boats ramming into *The Ariel* until it broke apart.

"I just can't bear the thought of not seeing her ever again," Flo whimpered. Was this how Joseph felt every day? She shook her head, trying to dislodge the horrible thoughts.

"But you will see her again." Flo felt Marianne's arm round her shoulders. "Just one more sleep. We'll arrive at the island tomorrow afternoon. We'll find Mum and bring her and her crew home."

Flo took a last look at *The Ariel* panel as the sub veered right and the seamount disappeared from view.

Then she made a mental checklist of things to do to keep busy. She'd look over the map one more time and check how Funmi was getting on with the radio repairs.

By tomorrow evening she would have her arms round Mum.

It was almost enough to reassure Flo.

Almost.

Chapter 23

JOSEPH TAKES THE WHEEL

"We've got a problem!"

Those were not words that Joseph wanted to hear right after having finished dinner. The warm feeling in his belly from the tomato soup he'd heated up on the stove vanished. He and Isaac jumped up from the table and rushed towards the control room. Flo and Funmi were already huddled around Marianne, all three staring at the control panel like it was about to bite them.

"What's happening?" Joseph looked out of the window; the light of the submarine cast a faint glow through the water, but he couldn't see anything to fear.

Until Marianne uttered three words.

"We're not alone."

"Is the satsuma ghost back?" Isaac asked.

Funmi shook her head. "It's something else."

Joseph saw a blue dot moving slowly towards them on the screen, growing larger with each pulse.

The submarine radio crackled with a muffled voice.

"They're trying to talk to us!" Joseph clamped his hand over his mouth. "Oh gills! Can they hear us?"

"No," Marianne replied. "Only if I hit the respond button. Let's sit tight for a minute."

The radio crackled again. This time the voice was clearer.

"I know you're there, Wanderdays. You got a good head start, but I'm afraid your best efforts have still fallen short. Turn back now."

"I recognize that voice!" Joseph gripped Flo's arm. "It's Linas! He's finally caught up."

His sister's face didn't reassure him like it usually did. Flo bared her teeth, but her bottom lip still quivered.

"What should we do?" Isaac asked.

A surge of courage ran through Joseph and he stepped forward. "How fast can this thing go?"

"Not sure." Marianne's green eyes glinted with intrigue. "But I'm keen to find out."

"You think we can lose Linas?" Funmi intervened. She shook her head like she was in a trance. "He's probably in some sort of super boat that runs on the tears of endangered animals. Flo, back me up here!"

"I—" Flo's unfinished sentence hung in the air. "I'm…not sure."

"This is your final warning!" the radio crackled again. "Turn back now and we'll chalk it up to Marianne de la Mer poisoning your impressionable little minds. Frederick will forgive your gross intrusion of privacy if you leave the island and his project well alone."

Joseph grabbed Flo's hands. He squeezed her palms tight and shook them, just like she had done for him so many times.

"What're you doing?"

"It's my turn now."

Flo blinked. "Your turn for what?"

"To be brave for both of us." Joseph hit the respond button on the control panel. "We're not scared of you and we're not turning back. Not until we find Mum."

His tongue tingled as adrenaline raced through his body. Had he just said that? The Joseph from last week would be hiding, buried in a book, face knotted with worry. He couldn't be that Joseph any more, not when

Mum was missing and in danger. And he hadn't been. The last few days had proved that his worries were not who he truly was. It had just been a while since he'd remembered that. He promised himself not to forget ever again.

"That was the wrong decision," Linas replied, his voice sharp as a coral edge. "Now we will sink you."

"They're getting closer!" Isaac flapped.

Through the window, Joseph saw the light of another submarine flashing in their direction. He looked at Marianne and they both understood each other. Joseph pressed the respond button a final time. "Only if you catch us first."

Marianne pulled a lever and the engine growled like a hungry beast. "Hold tight!"

Joseph grabbed Flo and pulled her down to the floor. The siblings huddled together, their knees touching and heads braced. Funmi and Isaac flopped down beside them just as the submarine flew through the water, like a rock catapulted from a slingshot.

Joseph had never been seasick before, but the speed at which Marianne navigated them through the water made his belly churn. Darkness enveloped the sub as it squeezed through a long coral arch. The metal hull scraped against the reef and Joseph winced as he saw a chunk of broken coral float past.

"I'm not sure we can outrun him!" Marianne veered sharply left. "Their submarine is fast."

"What should we do?" Flo sounded defeated.

Joseph got to his feet and staggered over to Marianne. "We need to hide!"

"Hide in the ocean?" she repeated, incredulous. "How?"

They zigzagged round a shiver of hammerhead sharks and Joseph gripped onto the back of the seat. He tried to block out the panic and focus on his thoughts. There had to be a solution. This was Dr Moray's research submarine, after all. Joseph scanned through his catalogue of memories until he landed on one.

"Isaac! Remember that podcast we listened to last month? With Dr Moray talking about his latest book?"

"Yeah!" Isaac's legs slipped from under him as he tried to pull himself up. "What about it?"

"He talked about the recent updates he'd made to his research sub." The answer was somewhere in the back of his mind, but Joseph couldn't grab onto it. "Do you remember?"

The beeping on the sonar screen grew louder. Linas was closing in.

"Erm." Isaac tapped his forehead. "Dr Moray talked about the extendable video arm that improved recording quality."

"That's not the one I'm thinking of." Joseph looked out as the water rushed past them. A kaleidoscope of colours, fishes and coral blended into one as Marianne steered the sub forward.

And that's when it hit him. The blending of colours, losing themselves in the ocean surrounds.

"It's camouflage!" Joseph said. "Dr Moray installed a camouflage shield so he could get closer to marine wildlife without disrupting their habitats."

"How do you camouflage an entire sub?" Funmi asked.

The question stumped Joseph. "Dr Moray said it was his special technology."

"But any idea how that technology works?" Flo was back on her feet, looking slightly more optimistic.

"However you do it, do it quickly!" Marianne slammed on the brakes and they all jolted forward as the submarine pulled into the entrance of a small cave. It wasn't deep enough for them to fully hide in. "They'll be on us in twenty seconds."

Joseph stared at the dozens of buttons and levers on the control panel. "There has to be something on here that activates it."

"What about this?" Isaac pointed to a small button at the bottom of the panel. It was shaped like an old soldier's shield.

"That has to be it." Joseph looked up at Isaac. "It's the only button that looks like a shield. That has to mean something. Right?"

"Ten seconds!" Marianne called.

Isaac nodded. "It makes sense. We trust your instinct. Do it."

Joseph hit the button. The shield symbol glowed white for a second, then disappeared.

"Has it worked?" Flo asked.

"I'm not sure." Joseph looked out of the window. The outside of the submarine didn't look any different. There'd been no loud mechanical noise or robot voice to confirm the shield was activated.

"We're about to find out!" Marianne silenced the engine. "Linas is here!"

The four friends linked arms as a dark shape emerged from the water. Joseph shivered when he saw the other submarine. The front was shaped like the prongs of a trident, with three pointed metal arms piercing the ocean. The main part of the submarine was as black as coal, its long, thin body moving through the water like a sea snake. It slowed down as it edged towards them. The radio stayed silent.

The trident submarine was almost within touching distance when it stopped abruptly and shifted to the left. As it did, Joseph spotted a large porthole on the submarine's side. He let go of the others and stepped towards the control-room window.

"What are you doing?" Flo hissed. "Come back!"

Joseph put his hands up to the glass and squinted to find Linas staring back at him. He gasped, the shock of it like a punch. Frederick Titan's right-hand man was looking straight at him, but there was no sign of recognition on his cold face.

"It's worked!" Joseph turned round to see the relief on his friends' faces. "He can't see us!"

When Joseph looked back, Linas was gone.

Moments later, the radio crackled.

"I've grown tired of your games. Frederick was willing to play nice, but now that's off the table. I hope you're ready to spend the rest of your days locked up along with your mother." He laughed. "See you on Fantome Island."

Linas's words echoed round the control room. The warning was clear. They'd ignored their one chance to turn back, but quitting had never been an option. Not when they were so close to getting Mum back. But Linas's taunt had also confirmed Joseph's suspicions.

"Our instinct was right." He turned to the others. "Mum and her crew made it to the island."

Marianne smiled at him, but it felt like a consolation. "I knew she would."

"But didn't you hear what else Linas said?" Flo balled her fists. "Mum is locked up. She and her crew are prisoners!"

"And Frederick knows we're coming now," Funmi said.

Isaac fiddled nervously with his Hamsa necklace. "So much for the element of surprise."

"We'll just have to be smarter and better then," Joseph said.

"And braver." Flo looked at him. "You think you've got enough courage for both of us?"

Joseph felt it in his bones before he'd even replied. "I've got an ocean's worth of the stuff."

Chapter 24

THE ARRIVAL

After the close call with Linas, Marianne waited until his submarine had dropped off the sonar screen before emerging from the cave. They continued their journey to Fantome Island, Marianne driving as fast as she could through the night to make up ground.

Flo tried to sleep, but it was impossible. Now that she knew Mum was a prisoner on the island, her mind ran wild picturing her chained up in a dark, damp cell. Frederick Titan had already destroyed so much to keep the island a secret and now he was holding Mum against her will. It made her boil with anger. Flo rolled onto her side and swung her legs over the edge of the bunk, scooping Zelda, her octopus, into her arms. Her feet had just touched the floor when she heard a stirring.

"Can't sleep either?" Joseph was sitting up on his bunk, notebook resting on his knees.

"No luck. Room for a little one?"

"You're not *that* little." Joseph shuffled over, holding up his blanket. "But sure."

Flo slipped in next to him and they turned to face each other.

"You were amazing earlier," she said. "How you stood up to Linas."

Even in the darkness, Flo sensed her brother's smile.

"When I heard his voice, something inside me shifted," Joseph replied. "I've spent so much time worrying over things I can't control. But hearing Linas taunt us like that. I should've been scared, but I wasn't. All I wanted to do was fight. I've been so used to worrying over things that *could* happen that I didn't realize how brave I could be with things that *are* happening."

"I wish Mum and Dad could hear you." Flo leaned across and ruffled his hair. "They'd be so proud."

Joseph yawned and rolled onto his side, taking the blanket with him. "I'll tell them myself when we're back home together."

"Sounds like a plan."

Soon after that, Flo heard the tiny nose whistles that her brother made as he fell asleep. She lay awake a while longer, wishing that Mum could hear her thoughts. *Hold on. Help is coming.* Flo's eyelids grew heavy and she finally fell asleep dreaming of Fantome Island and everything that waited for her there.

As the next morning drifted towards the middle of the day, Flo felt a shift of her own. She was sitting at the table next to Funmi, sharing a bag of plantain chips, when something pulled on her heart. She ran into the control room to find Marianne hunched over the screen.

"We're here, aren't we?" Flo asked.

"The island is just up ahead." Marianne beckoned her closer. "Right there."

Flo stared at the green blob on the sonar screen. It seemed so small and insignificant and she wondered how she could be so afraid of it.

There was a rustling sound behind her and Funmi popped her head round the door. "Have we arrived?"

Flo nodded just as Joseph and Isaac appeared below Funmi. They looked like floating heads and she quickly snapped a photo of them. She wanted to document the good and the bad of their journey.

"Can one of you go and send up the photonics mast?" Marianne asked. "I'll release some water from the tanks so we can get closer to the surface."

Flo frowned. "What's a *furtonic mask*?"

"Photonics mast," Marianne corrected her. "It's a periscope that captures images. We need to find a safe place to dock, somewhere isolated so we stay off-grid. Linas probably made it here before us and we don't want him to spot us approaching."

"I'm on it!" Flo hurried through the living quarters and down to the end of the passageway. She stepped onto a slightly raised platform and pressed a button overhead. The mast whirred as it slid upwards, like an antenna. "Sorted!" She raced back to the control room where the others stood round the larger screen.

"The images should be coming through any second now," Marianne said.

Anticipation crackled all around as the screen flickered into life. It took a moment for Flo's eyes to find what they were looking for but, when they did, excitement turned her dizzy. She leaned against Funmi to steady herself.

The island looked like a bruised fist that had punched its way to the surface; grey rocks clashed against a canopy of green and purple. In the middle of the island, Flo saw the apex of the volcano. It rose high above dense forest. She glanced at Joseph, who stared at the screen with an intensity she'd never seen. His lips were pursed like he was sizing up the island as an opponent before a fight.

"We made it," he said.

Flo set her jaw and prepared for what came next. When they reached the island, they would split up – one half heading to the laboratory and the other to the cabins – to search for Mum and her crew. Once they were reunited, they'd find the machine and uncover the truth about Project W.

Flo swore to herself that this would be Frederick's last ever scheme. He wasn't getting away this time. He was going to finally pay for the destruction he'd wrought across the world.

Despite the fear that pounded on her chest like a drum, she was ready for it all.

Chapter 25

(UN)WELCOME TO FANTOME ISLAND

Fantome Island was quiet, waiting for its new arrivals to make the first move. Mangrove trees stood strong like a first line of defence, wrapping themselves round the coast. The black sand was thick and the heat was sticky and oppressive, like someone had left an oven door open.

Joseph felt entirely unwelcome.

Once Marianne had located an isolated cove at the island's northern tip to surface the submarine, and had filled the ballast tanks with air, one by one they'd left through the hatch, swimming the short distance to the island shore.

Now they walked, rucksacks strapped to their backs,

across the sinking sand to the edge of the forest. Joseph's legs ached with each step.

"Alright?" Isaac asked.

"I've got that same feeling you get before an exam." Joseph clutched his stomach, his T-shirt already dry from the warmth of the sun. "Fizzy and fluttery. I can't believe we're here."

"I know." Isaac looked up as a flock of long-winged grey birds circled overhead. "I just keep picturing the look on my dad's face when he finds out where I am. He'd never expect me to do anything this wild." A speck of sadness appeared in his eyes. "Mum would've. She was always up for an adventure."

"How do you deal with it? That feeling of missing your mum all the time?" It was a question Joseph had long wanted to ask his best friend. Fear, of saying the wrong thing, had always stopped him before. "Does it ever go away? Sorry, that's a lot."

"No, it's okay." Isaac skirted round a sinkhole in the sand. "It comes and goes. When it's bad, I tell myself that the sadness is because I loved her so much. It's all of the extra love I still have for her." His chin wobbled. "Most of the time it makes me happy, but sometimes it's hard."

Joseph understood only a fraction of what Isaac felt. The last few days he'd felt something building up inside him. It was all of the love that he normally shared with Mum. It couldn't find an exit, not until he found her. "You can always talk to me, you know," he said. "Especially when it's bad."

Isaac looked out from under his fringe, his chestnut eyes glistening with almost-tears. "I know. Thanks."

"Get a move on, you two!" Funmi shouted. "No falling behind!"

Joseph and Isaac hurried to catch up. The others stood at the edge of the forest clearing where the skeleton of an old warehouse stood, its cracked windows frosted with ash.

"This wasn't on the map," Joseph said, startled.

Flo stepped through the door frame with her camera in hand. "Probably because there's nothing inside other than rubble and a lot of plants growing through the roof."

"The island is rewilding," Marianne said. "Nature is reclaiming the land."

Joseph looked at the dense forest and its interlocking leaves and trunks. It was still and silent. "What's the way from here?"

"There's a route that leads through the forest to the heart of the island," Flo said. "Once we clear the forest there are two paths. One leads to the cabins and the other leads to the lake and access to the volcano and the lab." Flo swatted a fly. "The path to the lab is harder though. And, as the volcano is on its own island within the lake, we'll have to find a way across the water."

Marianne tightened a camo utility belt round the middle of her black jumpsuit. "We'll need to stick to the shadows and find cover wherever we can. Linas is likely already here, but there's no knowing what or who else might be here. This is Frederick Titan's territory. We have to be alert at all times."

Everyone fell silent, the only noise the caws of the birds in the treetops.

"So to recap," Funmi's voice jangled with nerves, "we have to rescue your mum and her crew, although we don't know where they're being kept on the island. We have to find out what's going on inside the laboratory and what that weird machine is for. And we have to do all of that while basically trying to be invisible. Oh, and hoping the volcano is most definitely *not* active." She counted with her fingers. "Am I missing anything?"

Joseph took a deep breath. "One thing at a time.

That's how we face it. All of it."

He pulled back the leaves of an oversized sable palm and stepped into the forest.

The life of an explorer, Joseph realized, was much less glamorous than it sounded.

Even under the forest canopy, the heat made Joseph feel like he was walking in treacle. The initial path had quickly disappeared underneath vines and thick shrubs and they'd had to push themselves through bushes and climb round a suspected quicksand sinkhole. It had only been a couple of hours, but Joseph knew that every minute counted; they couldn't slow down or take a break. He mouthed the same word with each step he took. *Mum.*

"This heat is unbearable," Isaac moaned. He'd tied a spare T-shirt round his head and gained a stick somewhere along the way, that he used to clear his path. "How is it this hot in the shade?"

"I don't know, but we have to keep going." Flo wrung out the end of her ponytail.

The forest grew denser as time ticked on. Joseph's eyelids flickered and he took a long swig from his water bottle, pouring a few drops over his face. The cold re-energized him and he doubled his pace before breaking into a jog. He felt a pull on his heart, urging him to go faster. It was Mum, leading him to her.

"Don't go too far ahead," Marianne called.

And then, as if summoned by the power of thought alone, Joseph spotted an opening in the forest. The trees were beginning to part, gently trickling back like a tide rolling in to shore. They had almost reached the other side of the forest. Mum was closer than ever. His jog turned into longer strides and before he knew it, Joseph was sprinting, his rucksack thumping against his back.

"Joseph!" Flo's hissed whisper reached him. "Wait!"

But he couldn't wait. He'd done enough waiting. He had to get to Mum.

Adrenaline filled every part of Joseph. It rushed up his body and out through his ears, his eyes and mouth. The force of it propelled his legs through the gap in the trees until he was there, right at the edge of the clearing.

Joseph had been so sure that the ground would continue to exist under his feet that he hadn't thought to look down.

If he had, he might've seen the cliff edge from which he was about to fall.

Chapter 26

LIFE ON THE EDGE

Flo sprinted faster than she had at any Harbourview Academy athletics championship. Joseph had vanished from view and she feared the worst. Hadn't he remembered what she'd said about the forest? It was on higher ground. There was a drop.

The trees parted revealing the cliff edge, and Flo skidded to a halt. She dropped to her knees and shuffled towards the edge. She dug her fingers in between the cracks in the rocks and slowly lowered her head.

"Joseph!"

Her little brother hung from a branch jutting out of the cliff wall. Beneath him was a long drop leading to nothing but rocks. Flo batted away each thought of

Joseph growing tired, his fingers slowly uncurling from the branch. She stretched out one of her hands, but her fingers couldn't reach his.

"My arms are getting heavy," he whimpered. "I'm not sure I can hold on for much longer."

"Don't you *dare* let go!" Flo willed her fingertips to grow, but it was no use. She couldn't reach Joseph alone.

"What's going on?" Funmi and Isaac appeared beside her.

"Joseph fell. We need to pull him back up!"

"What?" Isaac gasped, before clearing his throat. "What do we do?"

"You need to lower me over the edge. I can reach him that way."

Marianne threw her rucksack on the ground and pulled out a small coil of rope. She unravelled it and threw one end to Funmi. "You and Isaac. Tie this around that tree trunk. As tight as you possibly can." She turned to Flo, looping and knotting the rope round her waist. "It really should be me doing this."

"It has to be me." Flo removed her camera from her neck and shrugged off her rucksack. "I'm lighter and I can keep him calm." She knew Marianne couldn't argue with that. Flo was Joseph's anchor.

"Good to go," Funmi called.

Marianne patted Flo's shoulder. "Now, slowly lower yourself over the edge."

"Flo! I'm slipping!"

Joseph's cries pained her as she shuffled closer to the edge. "I'm coming," she called back. "Just hold on."

Flo had never really been afraid of heights. She and Funmi had ridden every single roller coaster at the Aderemi Adventure Park multiple times. But this was different and, for all her toughness, fear fogged up Flo's brain like thick tendrils of smoke. She took a breath and asked her body to take over. She needed to do, not think.

Flo turned her back to the drop and lowered herself over the edge. Her stomach lurched, like it was about to fall out, but she didn't look down. If she did, the fear fog would spread. Loose rock crumbled around her, but she paid attention to her body, to the sting of her hands wrapped tight round the rope and her small measured footsteps. She tensed her toes, let her chest rise and fall, until she was parallel to the branch. Slowly, she looked away from her grip and focused on her brother.

The sight of Joseph was a gut punch. He was covered in cuts and scrapes and his rucksack dangled from his left shoulder.

“I’m here, Jojo.” She took a sideways step until she was close enough to the branch. She steadied herself and grabbed hold of his right wrist. He was sticky with sweat, but she gripped tighter, her nails digging in to his skin. She would not let go.

“On the count of three, I’m going to pull you in to me. Don’t resist, okay? I know you’re scared, but try and relax.”

“Relax!” Joseph squealed. “How?”

“Just don’t overthink, Jojo. I’ve got you.” She met his panicked eyes and all of Flo’s fear fog evaporated, replaced by an iron boldness. “One. Two.” Flo tensed every muscle in her body. “THREE!”

She swung towards Joseph and reached out for his left hand. Flo gripped it like a vice as he let go of the branch, and she pulled him in. The impact almost winded Flo, but she gritted her teeth. The pain had a purpose. The pain meant her brother was safe.

Joseph’s breaths tickled her skin. He’d attached himself to her back like a beetle shell and her muscles strained from the effort of holding him tight.

“I’ve got him!” she shouted. “Bring us up!”

The rope slowly lifted Flo and Joseph back up the cliff. Neither spoke. They just clung to each other, waiting to feel solid ground under their feet once again.

When they were level with the edge, Flo fell forward. She collapsed onto the ground with Joseph beside her. She heard Isaac sigh and felt Funmi's arms round her shoulders. Marianne rushed to Joseph and checked over his scrapes.

"I'm sorry. I don't know what came over me." Joseph's face twisted between relief and embarrassment. "I wasn't thinking about where I was. I was just thinking of Mum. It was reckless."

"It's okay," Flo replied. "But please don't run off again."

"Yeah," Isaac plucked a leaf from Joseph's hair. "We're a team."

"And we're a team who've made it to the heart of the island," Funmi said proudly. "Check out the view, you lot."

Now that her panic had settled, Flo spun round and looked out from the cliff edge. Properly. From here the map came to life. The volcano rose out of the ground like an ancient giant, surrounded by a lake with the bluest water she'd ever seen. As the map had indicated, the volcano was on its own little island in the middle of the lake.

"There's the laboratory!" Joseph pointed to a rectangular metal building at the foot of the volcano.

Flo grabbed her camera from her rucksack and hit record. She panned to three domed cabins on the other side of the lake, surrounded by a fence. They reminded her of igloos and she kept watch on their doors for a minute. No one came and went from them. All was quiet.

"I can't see any signs of life," she said.

Marianne nodded. "It's like a ghost town. That makes me nervous."

As Flo moved the camera back towards the lake, something new caught her eye. "What's that jutting out of the volcano?"

She zoomed in on a large glass lookout that had been built into the volcano's left-hand side. There were stairs leading up to it carved into the rock. The zoom on Flo's camera reached its max and the image turned grainy, but she'd seen enough to know that, whatever it was, it hadn't been marked on the island map. She passed her camera along, each one of them taking a look for themselves.

"It looks one of those fancy, all-glass, high-rise apartments in Brinemouth," Joseph said.

"Maybe it's Frederick's base when he comes to the island," Funmi offered.

Isaac nodded in agreement. "It is giving strong evil lair vibes."

Flo laughed nervously. "Whatever it is, we need to check it out. It could be another possible place he's keeping Mum."

As Funmi handed the camera back, a buzzing sound made Flo look up. A blue jay fluttered round their heads, its delicate black bill opening and closing. She offered an arm to the bird and it cocked its head before landing on her wrist.

"Hello, birdie." The blue jay hopped further up Flo's arm, but her smile disappeared when she looked into the bird's eyes. They were blood red and made up of tiny squares.

"Pixels," Flo muttered. She snatched her arm back and the blue jay fluttered to the nearest tree branch.

"What's going on?" Joseph asked.

"That bird," she said. "It's not real."

"What do you mean?" Funmi asked.

Before Flo could speak, the blue jay opened its bill. Instead of its usual sweet birdsong, a metallic screech reverberated through the air. Her hands flew up to her ears, but she still heard the words that felt like the end of everything.

"Intruder alert."

Chapter 27

THE SPLIT

Joseph landed in the bush with a thud. He'd scrambled away from the robotic bird and followed the others into the undergrowth. They crouched together and looked out through a gap between the leaves and thorns. The bird was flying in circles, its mechanical head snapping back and forth.

"What was that thing?" he whispered.

"The eyes," Flo said, wiping a hardened clump of dirt from her shin. "They were scanning me."

Funmi's mouth twitched. "Frederick really takes security measures to the extreme. Just what *is* happening on this island?"

That question hung in the air as all great, intimidating

questions do. Joseph knew they were all thinking of the lab and the machine – Frederick Titan's Project W.

After a minute, Joseph peered through the gap in the bush. The bird had stopped screaming, but there was a thin red light coming from its eyes. Flo was right. It was scanning the top of the cliff looking for intruders. Looking for them.

"We need to keep moving," Marianne instructed.

"There's a path leading down the cliff," Joseph said. "I saw it when I was, erm, dangling earlier. It's on the right, on the other side of these bushes. I can lead us there."

"That's the mark of a natural explorer." Marianne smiled at him. "Someone who's always alert, even when they're in trouble."

Joseph blushed. No one had ever called him an explorer before. Whenever he heard that word he thought of fearlessness, not stacks of worries higher than snow-covered mountain tops. But explorers were just people who possessed more curiosity than most and Joseph had always had that same desire to learn as much about the world as possible. So, actually, he *was* an explorer. He always had been.

They crawled out of the undergrowth and ran, backs

half bent, parallel to the edge of the cliff. Joseph checked over his shoulder with every chirp and rustle. The sky was clear and he could no longer see or hear the bird, but he didn't know whether that was a good or a bad thing.

Finally they reached the beginning of a sloping path. It was steep, with a narrow, uneven surface.

Isaac laughed nervously. "This looks fun."

"Just think of it like a water slide." Funmi secured her braids with her purple scrunchie. She offered a green one to Flo. "Scary on the way down, but once you reach the bottom you only remember how fun it was."

"But there's no water," Isaac replied.

Funmi rolled her eyes. "Use your imagination, Kessler. Who knows what sort of ladybirds and billion-legged bugs you'll see on the way down?"

"A billion? Please," Isaac said, exasperated. "The leggiest creature is the *Eumillipes persephone* and it still only has 1,306 legs."

They walked like crabs along the path, one by one, with their backs flat against the rocky walls. The rocks curved outwards at the top like a half roof. It wasn't much, but they were hidden from view and Joseph felt safe. As safe as an intruder could be on Fantome Island.

As they made their way down the slope, Joseph looked out at the volcano. It gave him a sense of fear and awe, like when he'd seen the satsuma ghost creature. The volcano was likely thousands of years old and had watched over the island for a long time.

A splash in the water drew Joseph's attention back to the lake and he wondered what other life lay beneath the surface. His eyes flitted between the lake and the laboratory and he thought of the machine and its individual compartments and helmets. Had the machine been designed for animals or humans? Or both? The thought made Joseph's skin crawl. He hated not knowing what Frederick's experiments were for, but now Joseph was closer than ever to uncovering the truth.

After twenty more minutes of navigating sharp bends and encouraging Isaac to keep going, they reached the end of the path. The ground evened out beneath their feet. To Joseph's left was the volcano lake. To his right was the cluster of cabins. Now that they were on level ground, Joseph could see the fence surrounding the cabins better. Whoever went in that direction would have to find a way through or over it.

"This way." Marianne beckoned them towards a nearby cluster of king palm trees.

When they had gathered underneath the trees, Funmi shrugged off her rucksack and pulled out the walkie-talkies. Marianne took one and clipped it to her belt.

"Right," Marianne said. "How are we doing this? Who's going where?"

Joseph opened his mouth, but Flo got there first. "You and I need to split up, Jojo. We can't make it easy for Linas to get his hands on both of us."

"You're with me then." Isaac looped an arm round Joseph's shoulder.

"Hang on." Flo's face was stern. "I think I should go with Isaac and Joseph with Funmi."

"But—"

"Your sister's right." Marianne nodded at him. "We all have different strengths and knowledge. The groups need to be balanced."

"Plus we're trusting each other with our best friends," Flo said. "That's no small task. That's everything."

"All settled then," Marianne said. "I'll go with Flo and Isaac to search the laboratory. Joseph and Funmi will head to the cabins. Finding Nellie and her crew is our priority, but keep your eyes peeled for anything that helps us make sense of the machine and what Frederick's Project W might be about."

Everyone nodded and said their goodbyes. When Flo looked at Joseph, he did his best to stop his top lip from wobbling.

"See you soon, bro."

"Very soon," Joseph whispered.

"Make sure you radio us once you reach the laboratory." Funmi waved her walkie-talkie at them.

"Will do!" Isaac said. "Make sure you say 'over' after every radio message. Over."

Joseph watched Marianne, Flo and Isaac run, half-crouching, out from the trees and towards the lake. He etched their figures into his mind. He didn't want to look away, but he forced himself to focus on what he now had to do. Joseph's eyes drifted across the field to the cabin enclosure, about a mile or so from where he stood, and gathered his courage.

He looked to Funmi and she looked back at him.

"Ready?" she asked.

Joseph nodded and the two of them broke cover, running away from the trees and into the open.

Chapter 28

WATER AND SKY MONSTERS

"My ear's full of water! Help!"

Flo grabbed the scruff of Isaac's T-shirt. "That's normally what happens when you dunk your head underwater!"

Swimming across the lake had been the only way to reach the laboratory and stay out of sight of the robo-birds flying above their heads. Flo used her rucksack like a float to stay above water, but Isaac was somehow failing spectacularly.

"But I was looking for the *Anisosticta novemdecimpunctata*!" He coughed up a lungful of lake water.

"Come again?"

"A water ladybird with bright yellow elytra. I saw one on that reed."

"I'd rather you didn't drown for the sake of a ladybird," Marianne called from the front. "Come on, we've almost reached the other side."

As Isaac chopped through the water using his best doggy-paddle, Flo kicked her legs and looked up at the volcano with each stroke. It loomed large and made everything feel insurmountable, but when she thought of Mum her resolve hardened like magma. The motivation to find her was at the heart of everything. Still, Flo couldn't deny the small thrill she felt at uncovering the secrets in the laboratory and exposing Frederick's true self. She'd capture it all on film, as long as her camera survived the swim in her waterproof rucksack.

Flo pushed on with aching muscles until the edge of the volcano island was within reach. With a helping hand from Marianne, she pulled herself onto the shore. She turned round to help Isaac, but a big splash from the middle of the lake drew her attention. She saw a long figure just below the surface heading towards Isaac. Its movements were sharp and jerky, stopping and starting as it made its way across the lake.

“Grab my hand!” Flo urged. “There’s something in the water.”

“What?” Isaac began to panic. “What is it?”

“I don’t know. Just grab my hand and I’ll pull you up.”

Isaac reached for her hand, but his fingers slipped through hers.

“Try again!” she urged.

Isaac reached again, but it was no use. His hands were too wet.

In one moment Marianne was by Flo’s side. The next, she’d dived into the lake. Flo tried to track every movement, but the water thrashed like it was fighting itself. She dropped to her knees and waited.

When it arrived, Flo didn’t mind the great wave of water that soaked her. Marianne emerged, one arm wrapped around Isaac’s chest, as she pulled him to shore.

“Get his arms!”

Flo stretched out and wrapped her hands round Isaac’s arms. She heaved him out of the water. “Are you okay?” She rubbed his back and water spurted from his mouth like a fountain. “What was that?”

“I’m alright.” Isaac coughed. “I couldn’t see much,

but I felt hands grip my waist before Marianne jumped in. But the hands weren't normal, Flo. They felt rough. Almost scaly."

Isaac's description of the hand in the water reminded Flo of the science-fiction films that Dad put on when he thought she was fast asleep. The images of strange creatures and monsters she'd watched through the crack in the movie-room door set her mind racing about the creatures she'd already seen on Fantome Island. "Maybe the robo-birds are part of Project W. And the same for whatever that thing was in the lake."

"The answers are in reach now." Marianne wrung the water from her hair and helped Isaac to his feet. "We've made it to the lab."

Flo threw on her rucksack and got to her feet. Turning away from the lake, she saw the laboratory building at the foot of the volcano. The lab had been built to blend in with the surrounding piles of obsidian rock, its metal facade a shiny black. There were no windows, only the outline of a narrow door. Nearby vents spouted steam and a sharp acrid smell stung her nostrils.

"Frederick's reign of doing what he wants ends today," Flo said, anticipation coursing through her. "I—"

A loud noise cut her off. It had crept up on them, gentle at first, like the thrumming of bees in summertime. Then the sky rumbled and a roaring sound filled Flo's ears. Her hair whipped across her face and Funmi's green scrunchie flew into the lake. The wind made it hard to move, but Flo forced her head up and she saw a great metallic monster in the sky. "A helicopter!"

Marianne nodded towards the rocks. "We need to take cover."

Flo slung her arm round Isaac's shoulders and they hurried after Marianne, throwing themselves to the ground behind the obsidian. The smell from the lab vents was even stronger here and Flo cupped her mouth as she followed the helicopter's path in the air. It veered to the left and hovered above the glass lookout. The sunlight hit the helicopter's tail rotor and it sparkled golden, like a prized piece of jewellery.

"That's the helicopter we saw at Titan Towers," Flo breathed. "It's him. Frederick's here."

"So he's decided to show up and get his own hands dirty," Marianne muttered. She cracked her knuckles, which made a loud pop.

"I think he's trying to land on top of the lookout."

Isaac craned his neck. "He's flying right towards the glass."

"There's no point sitting around while that happens." Flo indicated the laboratory in front of them. "We're so close now!" She checked the sky again for any sign of the robo-birds. "Let's go."

Flo bolted towards the door, checking all around for any hidden cameras nestled in between the rocks. She tried not to let the roar of the helicopter distract her from their mission.

Marianne swept her hands across the door frame. "I can't see any alarms on this thing."

Flo reached out and slowly pushed against the door, but it didn't budge.

Marianne pulled a silver rectangle from her belt; ten different wires stuck out from the sides like spider legs. She crouched level with the lock. "Let's see how quickly I can pick this."

Flo watched her flit between the wires, twisting them in the lock until she heard a click. A high-pitched click seemed to signal progress. A dull click meant better luck next time.

"It's all about finding the right pressure point." Marianne continued to work. There was a whining click and she stood up, triumphant, and gave the door a gentle nudge. It opened a fraction.

Flo stepped in front of Marianne and hesitated on the door's threshold. She had no idea what awaited them on the other side.

"Do it," Isaac said, his hands wrapped around his necklace.

"We're right behind you," Marianne added.

Flo pushed the door all the way open, a waft of strong chemicals seeping out, and stepped inside the laboratory.

Chapter 29

A CLOSE SPIKE

Joseph felt entirely exposed as he and Funmi ran across the dull, dark-green grass field. Out here in the open there was nowhere to hide from watching eyes.

Fantome Island wasn't a typical tropical island, with golden sand, bright green grass and thriving wildlife. It was beautiful in its own way, with its jagged cliff edges, rocky terrain and sparkling lake water, but it was dangerous. So very dangerous. Joseph wouldn't forget that.

Every time they heard the mechanical squawk of a robo-bird, they dropped to the ground until the birds flew off again. The field felt never-ending, but the flat land soon turned into thick bracken that Joseph and

Funmi waded through like a swamp. Rough branches and thorns scraped against them, but they pushed on. The cabins inched closer with every step.

"All of the shea butter in the world won't save my skin." Funmi clawed at her arm like an angry cat as she flicked a purple-veined leaf off.

"There's not much further to go." Joseph pushed through a large branch. "Now we just need a way to get past the fence."

"It's much higher than I thought." Funmi peeled back the last fern and they stepped into a circular clearing. The giant grey fence stared back at them like a challenge.

"Let's do a lap," Joseph said. "There might be a gap that we can squeeze through somewhere."

They fell into step together, cautiously glancing in opposite directions every few seconds.

"The silence is freaking me out," Funmi whispered. "I thought there'd be people here. Noise. Something."

Joseph nodded. "I don't trust it either."

They were halfway round the fence when Joseph spotted a way in. There was an empty space between two sections of the fence, as though it had been left unfinished.

"Nice!" Funmi grinned.

Inside, the three domed cabins were arranged in a semicircle. One of them had a large antenna poking out of its roof and a red beacon flashing at its top. A feeling of unease grew inside Joseph. Why did the cabins have high-end security measures when the fence was incomplete? It didn't make any sense. Joseph was so distracted by this that he almost missed Funmi's mistake.

"Wait!" He pulled her back by her rucksack straps as she was about to walk through the empty space. "Something's not right."

Funmi frowned. "What do you mean?"

"It seems too easy. Everything about Frederick Titan's security has been pretty high-tech," Joseph reasoned. "If he's keeping Mum in one of these cabins, or even the machine, it doesn't make sense. He wouldn't keep his secrets so unprotected."

"In his house, yes. But Fantome Island *is* his secret."

Funmi continued talking, but Joseph was distracted by a butterfly moving towards the gap. It flew through it and, as quick as a blink, something sharp shot out from each side of the fence. It clipped the butterfly's wings and it fell to the ground. White-green foam pooled round the fallen insect.

Funmi cupped her hands to her mouth. "What happened to it?"

Joseph slowly shuffled forward, staying in the shadow of the fence. If anyone was in the cabins he didn't want to be spotted now.

"I think it's been poisoned." Lying next to the butterfly was a long, thin arrow. The tip of the arrow was made up of lots of smaller spikes. They were a dull white colour.

"Oh my gills!" Joseph fell back. "This is a pufferfish-spike arrow. Funmi, it could've killed you."

"Huh?"

"Pufferfish are deadly. Their spikes carry a poison called tetrodotoxin, which can kill other animals. Humans too."

"Oh." Funmi's face dropped at the news of her close brush with death. "Good looking out, Jojo."

"We need to climb over the fence. That's the only way we're getting to the cabins." He looked around, but there were only plants and fallen branches scattered over the floor. "Any ideas?"

Funmi raised her chin as she surveyed their surroundings. "I know," she said decidedly. "We'll make a ramp."

"From what?"

"Nature, obviously."

The heavy, makeshift ramp didn't fill Joseph with confidence. He'd followed Funmi's instructions and tied multiple branches together with thick vines and the string cord from his rucksack. Together, they propped it up against a back section of the fence. All three cabins faced one direction and, this way, they'd be able to climb over the fence without being noticed. Hopefully. Joseph had nothing but hope for what they were about to do.

"I'll go first," Funmi said. "Only fair considering it was my idea."

"Be careful!" Watching Funmi climb up the ramp set Joseph's nerves on high alert. He winced every time her foot slipped. The middle part of the ramp wobbled and he thought it was about to come crashing down, but it held as Funmi scrambled to the top of the fence. She swung her legs over, checked the other side of the fence, and signalled a thumbs up. It was Joseph's turn.

He gripped the sides and dug his feet into the natural groove of the branches. Joseph moved slowly, concentrating on where he placed his hands and how much pressure each foothold could take. He smelled resin, sweet and sticky, as the branch widened in the middle. He stayed low, keeping his body streamlined, and crawled higher until he felt his hand reach the top of the concrete fence. He reached up for Funmi's hand and she pulled him onto the fence beside her.

"Impressive balance. You should join the school climbing team!"

"Team sport isn't really my thing." Joseph looked down at the ground and his belly lurched. "Not a fan of heights either."

"You might continue to surprise yourself." Funmi grabbed the top of the ramp. "Help me pull this over. We need it to get down on the other side."

Joseph's muscles ached under the weight of the ramp, but together they managed to slide it over the other side of the fence. He surveyed the cabins below as he helped Funmi fix the ramp in place. Joseph could hear a noise now, quiet chatter coming from the furthest cabin. A light flickered on in its window.

"Someone's inside!"

Funmi pursed her lips. "Then let's shimmy down this thing as fast as we can."

Once their feet touched solid ground on the other

side of the fence, Joseph let out a small sigh of relief. It only lasted a second before he grabbed Funmi's hand and ran towards the closest cabin. They crouched low behind the back window for cover.

"We should check in with the others," he whispered. "See how they're getting on."

Funmi grabbed the walkie-talkie from her rucksack and pressed the button. "Flo. Isaac. Marianne. Does anyone read us? Over."

Joseph waited for the walkie-talkie to crackle. With each passing second that it didn't, his nerves climbed higher in his throat. "Try again."

"Does anyone copy?" Funmi tried again in a hushed tone. "We're at the cabins and about to enter. Over."

The radio hissed with static. No reply came.

Joseph's face creased in half. "Do you think they're in trouble?"

"They're with Marianne. I'm sure they're safe."

Joseph's fingers itched with the familiar longing to click. "You're right. They'll call when they can."

"But I do have some good news!" Funmi smiled.

"What?"

She pointed above their heads to the window's latch. It was unlocked. "That's our way in."

Before Joseph could reply, Funmi had grabbed the window frame and pushed it up, leaving a gap wide enough to fit through. She went first, effortlessly twisting her body through the space.

"Funmi!" he hissed. "Wait for me."

"Hurry up." She stuck her hand back out the window to help pull him through.

Joseph landed with a thud on the wooden floor next to Funmi.

They were inside the cabin.

Chapter 30

A DOUBLE DISCOVERY

The laboratory door swung shut behind them and darkness wrapped around Flo like a blanket.

"Hopefully this means no one else is in here," she whispered. There were footsteps next to her and then a crashing sound, followed by a grunt of frustration.

"Ouch!" Isaac yelped. "I just walked into something sharp."

"Hang on." Flo shrugged off her rucksack and searched through it, feeling for the shape of her torch. She felt the cold metal and moments later the torch illuminated the laboratory.

"Let's search this place together," Marianne said.

The inside of the laboratory was all silver and the

overhead lights glistened off the steel table surfaces. Flo shone the torch across the room, her heart in her throat at the thought of coming across one of Frederick's scientists. They couldn't get caught now. Trolleys and chairs were lined up in a uniform row and the cabinets that lined the walls held glass jars of strange specimens: fish gills, multicoloured fins and variously sized eyeballs. There were posters of human anatomy and intricate-looking graphs plastered along one wall; one was of a human body, although with a tail instead of legs.

Flo held the torch steady as Marianne and Isaac crawled under the tables, checking every nook and cranny of the lab. But there was no one there. No Mum, no scientists. It was all so quiet. Too quiet.

"I can't see anything in here that looks like the machine." Marianne's voice was hardened with disappointment. "We need to keep looking."

They walked the length of the lab, inspecting every table and cabinet. Flo's own frustration grew. With each step she felt even further away from finding Mum, finding the machine and unravelling the mystery of Fantome Island.

Until her torchlight landed on a piece of paper pinned underneath a silver tray on one of the tables. In a place so clinical and carefully arranged, it seemed out of place. She wriggled it free and turned it over.

"*The Weaver*," Flo repeated. "*The how-to manual for human adaptation against the climate crisis*." All of the words were familiar to her, but together in one sentence they read like a cryptic clue she couldn't crack. There was something else even more familiar to Flo.

"This handwriting." She looked at the delicate outward flicks of the letter W. "I recognize it."

Isaac peered over her shoulder. "Isn't it Frederick's?"

"No," Flo replied. "It's not his. It's someone else's, but I just can't remember where I know it from." Deep in thought, she allowed Isaac to gently pull her back over to the poster of the fish-person on the wall.

"What about this?" he asked. "Do you think this is the thing that attacked me in the lake?"

Flo stopped studying the handwriting and looked up at the poster. Under the fish-person specimen was a sentence: *Test model ten: adaptable for land and water living*.

"It's possible," she said. "This has to be Frederick's secret project. Making these half-human, half-amphibian *creatures*." She turned on her camera and took a sweeping shot of the laboratory, before zooming in on the poster. The fish-person's hands were scaly, just like the hands that had grabbed Isaac in the lake.

"But why?" Isaac rubbed his head. "Why would he do this?"

It was a question that Flo couldn't yet answer. She thought of the figure swimming near the lake's surface and how it had looked humanlike. From her uncertainty came a new question, one that turned her mouth dry and her skin cold. "Do…do you think he'd experiment on Mum and her crew? Maybe that's why he's keeping them as prisoners. Because he needs test subjects!"

Isaac's face was blank. "I don't think…" He trailed off. "I don't know, to be honest. But I promise we'll find her before anything bad happens."

But it was a promise he couldn't keep. Suddenly the laboratory felt blurry as Flo's mind swam with visions of Mum trapped inside the Project W machine, hooked up to wires. Flo leaned against a cabinet to steady herself, but it moved behind her and she fell back, bracing herself for the impact against the metal wall.

It didn't come.

Instead there was only space and air behind her and she continued to fall until Isaac grabbed her arm and pulled her forward. She landed on the laboratory floor with a bump, keeping her camera above her head so it didn't smash against the tiles. The torch clattered to the floor and Flo winced at the noise.

"What happened?" Marianne rushed towards them. "Are you alright?"

Isaac smiled. "More than fine."

"Speak for yourself." Flo rubbed her arm. "Why do you look so pleased?"

"Look behind you."

Flo spun round. There was a door-shaped hole in the wall that led to a spiral stone staircase. The cabinet had been blocking it. "Another passageway," she said, her hope reigniting.

Marianne helped Flo to her feet and grabbed the torch. "Get behind me. I'll lead the way."

Flo gripped Isaac's shoulders as they followed Marianne down the staircase, below ground level. The steps were narrow and the three of them stuck close to the wall.

"Are we inside the volcano now?" Flo whispered. Her arms ached, but she didn't dare let go of Isaac.

"Maybe," he replied. "Either way we're definitely underground. Nothing on this island is what it seems."

"Careful!" Marianne called. "A couple of these next steps are crumbling."

Flo had counted three hundred and twenty steps by the time the staircase came to an end. It opened up into a large, bright chamber, big enough to hold an entire cathedral. Flo looked up and saw natural light streaming in from a hole above them. It took her a second to realize that the hole was the open volcano mouth.

"We *are* inside the volcano!"

The chamber walls changed colour depending on where Flo stood. She saw shades of yellow, green, purple and dark red splattered across the rock. "How is this even possible?" Of all the feelings that burgeoned inside her, awe broke through.

"This volcano must've erupted before," Marianne explained. "The magma can retreat underground and harden into rock to create chambers like this."

"Wow." Flo's hands couldn't move fast enough as she clicked record on her camera. The chamber was one of the most incredible things she'd ever seen. Nature was like that, terrifying and beautiful at the same time. The entire journey to Fantome Island had been much the same.

"Psst!" On the other side of a stalagmite Flo saw Isaac

crouched low behind a rock wall. "Over here," he whispered.

She ran towards him, kicking up clouds of rock dust with her speed. Flo snuck in next to Isaac, with Marianne on the other side, and looked over the wall. Flo's hands flew to her mouth, stifling her gasp.

"The machine," she whispered, her voice muffled. "We've found it."

The glass tank was tall and narrow. Just like the blueprint, it was divided into four compartments with four dangling helmets. Flo followed the wires that spouted out of the helmets to a smaller black box sitting at the foot of the machine. There, Flo saw two scientists in lab coats and goggles sitting at a workbench. One of them was looking down a microscope. The other was slotting a Petri dish into the top of the black box.

"What is this?" Isaac whispered.

"Flo," Marianne hissed. "You need to record this."

Placing her camera on top of the rock wall, Flo looked down the lens. She zoomed in on the table, but she couldn't get a clear picture of what was under the telescope or what was inside the Petri dish. "We're too far away. We need to get closer."

Just as Flo was about to jump the wall, the scientist with the telescope looked up sharply. She flung herself back, praying she hadn't been spotted.

"The next sample is ready," the same scientist said. "Prepare the Weaver for the test on Subject Two."

"Preparations underway," the other scientist confirmed. "I'll radio the cabins now and instruct them to bring the subject."

"The Weaver," Flo repeated. Her lungs were full of dust and she tried to swallow down her cough. "That's the name of the machine! Project W. Project *Weaver*."

Isaac scrambled in his rucksack and found the walkie-talkie. "They're heading to the cabins! Joseph and Funmi are probably already there. We need to warn them!"

"It's too late for that, I'm afraid," a voice said, deep and gleeful, from behind them.

Before Flo could respond, a net fell over her head. It trapped her like a web and knocked her to the ground. She tried to move, but the rope was too heavy.

"Flo?" Isaac called. "What's happening?"

"Stay calm!" Marianne's voice sounded far away.

All Flo could do was stare at the chamber floor and the walkie-talkie just out of reach on the other side of the net. She heard a low chuckle before something moved over her face and she was plunged into total darkness.

Chapter 31

COMING OUT OF A CAGE

Joseph's eyes adjusted to the darkness of the cabin room. His nose, however, refused to adjust to the smell of thick chlorine and rotting damp. It turned his belly queasy.

"Hello?" He took a cautious step forward, Funmi by his side. "Anyone here? Mum?"

"Joseph!" someone called out from the pitch black. "Is that you?"

"Sal!" He recognized the voice of *The Ariel*'s cook instantly. "Where are you?"

"Don't turn the light on!" Sal replied. "The switches are rigged to the security system."

"Hang on." Funmi pressed a button on her watch and its torch illuminated the large animal cage that took up most of the room. Joseph spotted people slowly pushing themselves up from the floor. Their faces became clearer. He saw some of Mum's crew – Mona, Belle, Indira and Sal. The rest of the crew had to be here too inside the cage, Mum included. The belief pushed him forward.

Joseph twisted his arms through the bars. "We're going to get you all out of here."

"You brilliant boy." Sal gripped his hands tightly. Their bright coral hair was faded and dark semicircles hung like crescent moons under their eyes. "How on earth did you get here?"

"We – us two, Flo and Isaac – came with Marianne. Mum's old friend. She told us all about the *real* Frederick Titan and we knew you were in danger. We came to bring you home.

"Plus, we borrowed Dr Moray's submarine." Funmi grinned. "That's how we actually got here."

"Nellie said Marianne would keep watch over you, but I don't think she expected a rescue mission. None of us did." Sal rubbed their eyes. "This island is dangerous."

"We know." Joseph stood on his tiptoes, stretching to see the back of the cage. "Where's Mum?"

The little light left in Sal's face went out like a blown

fuse. "We've not seen Nellie since we arrived. They took her away somewhere else."

Tears came rushing down Joseph's cheeks like a flood. "Mum!" He ripped his hands from Sal's and hugged his body, trying to keep himself together. How could he have come so far, been through so much, and still not found Mum?

"We're going to find her." Funmi's voice was soft yet forceful. "We're not leaving this island until we do, okay?"

Joseph nodded through his sobs. "What happened?"

"We were looking for the island when we received a distress signal from another boat." Sal sucked their teeth. "Naturally, your mum instructed that we help. By the time we found the other boat, it was too late to realize it was a trap. We were boarded."

Joseph shook his head, trying to dispel the image of Mum rushing to someone's help, only to realize it was a trick.

"Turns out Frederick had paid pirates to come after us. They tied us up on their boat, then they rammed right into *The Ariel*. Broke the hull apart. It's lost to the ocean now." Sal sniffed. "Anyway, the pirates dumped us on the island shore. That's when we were separated from Nellie. People in white coats took her away, but she didn't go without a fight. You can bet she's still giving them hell."

Joseph knew Mum's spirit was hard to break, but she was still human. He prayed that they'd find her before she reached her limit.

"A man came in with one cup of water and a piece of bread not too long ago," Sal added, "but we've not seen anyone else."

Funmi dropped to her knees by the lock and dumped her rucksack on the floor. "We better not waste any time in getting you all out. Do you know if this cage is rigged?"

Indira, *The Ariel*'s engineer, appeared next to Sal. "We only know about the lights because the man earlier had to deactivate a code by the door before flipping the switch. So it might be, but it also might not."

"Excellent." Funmi held her tongue between her teeth. "Only one way to find out then." She grabbed her pocket knife and began to twist one of its small blades through the cage lock. The last of Joseph's nerves were at breaking point and he waited for the sound of a blaring alarm or heavy footsteps running in his direction. The only sound that he did hear was the click of an opening lock. He cheered quietly as the cage door sprang open and out poured all of Mum's crew. They crowded round him and Funmi, wrapping them in a great hug. He passed Sal his water bottle and Funmi handed out the remaining tamarind balls, which the rest of the crew devoured.

Joseph was far from Brinemouth, but this moment felt like a little bit of home.

Until the door to the cabin swung open and the room was bathed in bright artificial light.

"Well, well, well."

Feeling his belly drop, Joseph did his best not to flinch at the unwelcome voice. He rubbed his eyes and saw Linas standing in the cabin doorway. Four men stood either side of him. They were dressed in long white coats and held large scalpels in their hands.

Linas twisted his mouth into a sneer. "Looks like we have a jailbreak on our hands."

Chapter 32

CAUGHT IN A TITAN TRAP

Flo woke to the sound of water. Her head throbbed and she tried to sit up, but kept slipping back down. She felt the rope underneath her and realized she was still trapped inside the fishing net. Somehow the net was no longer on the floor but suspended from the ceiling. Flo looked around. She wasn't in the chamber, she was in a different room. How had she got here? Her hands moved to her stomach, relieved to feel the familiar shape of her camera tucked under her T-shirt, but her rucksack was gone.

There was a bubbling sound beneath Flo and she looked down to see a circular, man-made pool. The water rippled and, as she looked beyond the pool, Flo realized where she was. She saw the huge glass window on the other side of the room that looked out onto the island.

She was inside the lookout.

The glass room was almost homely, with a long white sofa and a round chrome table. A messy desk overlooked a wall of bookcases. A doorway led to the stairs outside, which had been built into the side of the volcano. Flo could only see the top steps through the window and she wondered how high up they were. She rubbed her head, her memories hazy. One moment she'd been inside the chamber watching the scientists prepare the Weaver machine, then everything had gone dark and now she was here. A prisoner.

"Flo?"

She turned round, the net swinging back and forth with her jerky movements. Isaac was behind her in another net. "Thank Oceanus!" Flo wished she could reach out and hug him. "Are you alright?"

"No." Isaac whispered something like a prayer. "Where's Marianne?"

Flo scanned the rest of the lookout room, but Marianne was nowhere to be seen. "I don't know, but we've got to get out of here." She calculated the distance between the net and the stone floor. "If I can find something to cut through the rope, I can break apart one of the holes and jump. I should be able to clear the pool from here."

Isaac looked at her like she'd suggested pole-vaulting over the moon. "Alright for you. You're tall *and* athletic! There's no way I can make that."

"I'll get down and find another way to free you."

"Don't you dare leave me behind!"

Flo sighed. "I'm not going to leave you. I need to figure out how to cut through this first. Do you still have your rucksack?"

"No. Whoever captured us must've taken it. You got yours?"

Flo shook her head. Her panic grew, but she tried not to let it show. "I'll find a way to get us out of here. Just try not to look down. And remember to breathe."

"That's not helpful," Isaac replied. "Like I'm going to forget how to do the most basic bodily function. I— Oh my great gills!" Underneath his net the pool bubbled and Isaac clawed at the rope, desperate to climb higher.

"I told you not to look down!"

"But we're going to be eaten alive! By piranhas!"

"They're stonefish, actually." A familiar voice echoed

around the room and Flo's head jerked back. "Stonefish are the most venomous fish known to man. They only sting when threatened, but I'd say two insufferable children falling into their water is enough to make them mad."

Isaac whimpered. Fear turned Flo's mouth dry, but she refused to be scared of Frederick Titan any longer.

"You've got yourselves into a pickle, haven't you?" Frederick emerged from the lookout doorway. Gone were the signs of old age that Flo had noticed at Titan Towers. On Fantome Island Frederick looked alert and alive, with a face full of venom. "I imagine your brother and the Aderemi girl are here too." He tutted. "What a terrible waste of such promising lives."

"Let us go!" Flo clawed at the net. She spotted a small remote with a red button in Titan's left hand and wondered what it was for. Likely nothing good. "The police are on their way here right now," she said. "This island will be swarming with officers."

"Oh, Florence." Frederick chuckled. "Your fake threats are about as scary as a bunny rabbit. Fantome Island is a ghost. The only map here is the one you so rudely looked at without permission. The police will never find it."

"Where's Mum?" Flo growled. "Where's her crew? What have you done with Marianne?"

"Aren't you full of questions?" Frederick halted at the pool's edge. "They're all alive, for now, although Marianne is currently being prepped for our next experiment. A late but excellent addition." He grinned and wagged a finger at Flo. "I had a suspicion that Marianne would reappear and attempt to poison your minds. It's a shame she succeeded. I thought you were smarter than that."

"We *are* smarter than that!" Flo's body trembled as she failed to pull herself upright again. She concentrated on making her voice bold and brave. "Marianne told us the truth about your double life. You're no Earth-hero. You don't care about stopping the climate crisis. You never did. Creating The Titans and the TV show – it was all just a cover-up so you could travel the world and fill your pockets. Whatever you're doing on this island with your latest project is no different."

"So many people looked up to The Titans." Isaac had found his voice. "It was all a lie. You only ever wanted to help yourself."

"People are always looking for something to believe in –" Frederick knelt slowly at the pool edge. He took a barely wriggling fish from his pocket with his free hand and tossed it into the air. A sharp, stony fin cut through the water and a gaping open jaw emerged. "– so they turned to The Titans, with me as their god." He smiled as the stonefish devoured its prey. "It was one of my greatest creations. People looked to me to tell them how to save our planet. I offered them hope."

Anger flooded every part of Flo. All she could see and hear was a man who was motivated by one thing. Greed. As long as he was adored and his pockets were full, Frederick didn't care if the world burned around him.

"False hope!" Isaac shouted. "You told them how to look after our planet while you were destroying it!"

Flo gave up trying to stand. She watched Frederick walk towards Isaac's net and quickly lifted the bottom of her T-shirt, positioning her camera between her knees before hitting record. Even if she couldn't get a good view of Frederick, her camera would capture the audio. She needed a recording of his confessions, the final nail in his coffin.

"When everyone finds out the truth, it'll be over," Isaac continued. "No one will ever think of you as a god. Your name will mean nothing."

“I’ll just make sure that no one else finds out the truth.” Frederick waved the remote mockingly. “All I have to do is press this button and you’ll be stonefish supper. Then I just have to deal with the remaining troublemakers. If Linas hasn’t already taken care of them.”

Flo snarled in response. She desperately hoped Joseph and Funmi were okay and that Mum and her crew were holding up. But Frederick had said Marianne was being prepared for the next experiment and surely that was something he would oversee? Flo had to keep Frederick talking, to buy them time until an escape plan emerged. The only way she could do that, Flo knew, was to use her curiosity.

“What’s the Weaver for, anyway? We know all about it and what you’re doing, but what we don’t understand is why. Why are you making these *creatures*? If you’re going to feed us to your stonefish then why not share your secret?”

“Flo!” said Isaac through chattering teeth. She moved an arm behind her back, hoping her thumbs up would convey all that he needed to know. *Trust me. I’m trying to save us.*

“You’re certainly as bold as your mother, I’ll give you

that." Frederick licked his top lip, as though savouring the thought.

Flo commanded her face to hide the disgust she felt.

"The Weaver is a one-of-a-kind machine that will transform life as we know it. Its technology will allow humans to live longer, to adapt to whatever challenges the changing climate and planet throw our way. It is a marvel, truly, that will cement my place in history for ever. But I cannot take full credit for its creation. Oh no." Frederick's face softened slightly. "I required the brightest scientific mind I've ever known."

Flo frowned. "Who?"

"The nets are rather over the top," another voice interrupted. "Can't you let them down, Frederick?"

Flo clasped her hands to her mouth. The sudden jerk of her arms knocked her camera onto its side. Frederick stared at her before turning to meet the person now standing in the lookout doorway.

Hope had arrived in the form of a voice that Flo hadn't heard in years.

Uncle Percy was alive.

And he was here on Fantome Island.

Chapter 33

FACE-OFF

Joseph quite liked the odds. He, Funmi and Mum's crew made nine, so it was a simple mathematical equation that the odds of beating Linas and the scientists were in their favour. But staring at their cold, vicious faces and the glistening scalpels in their hands made Joseph feel that getting past them and out of the cabin would be anything but simple.

"A valiant attempt." Linas stepped towards them and ran his hands along the cage bars. "You might even have got away with it too, if I hadn't spotted your pathetic makeshift ladder on the security camera. I thought I'd give you a head start, so you could at least find this motley crew before I came and spoiled the party."

"You monster!" Sal cracked their knuckles. "You'll pay for this."

The rest of Mum's crew cried in agreement. Their shouts rallied Joseph and he took a bold step forward. "Where's Mum? Where are you keeping her?"

"Why would I ever tell you that?" Linas and the scientists laughed together.

"Because if you don't," Funmi said, "it'll be you in that cage."

"I very much doubt that. You may outnumber us but we have an advantage." Linas's pupils spilled into the whites of his eyes. "Nellie is about to go to the Weaver. She's the star of our next experiment. It's too late."

The scientists closed in like a pack of hunters round their prey and Joseph's mind scrambled, trying to understand what Linas had just said. What was the Weaver? If it was a part of the experiments, did that mean it was linked to the machine? Was the Weaver the machine?

A piercing scream shook the cabin and every thought of Joseph's fell away apart from one. *Mum.*

"It's Mum!" His heart had recognized the sound quicker than his ears. "She's close by!" Joseph flared his nostrils at Linas. "And that's where you're wrong. It's never too late to save the people you love."

Joseph cried out loud and ran head first at Linas and the scientists. If he couldn't get past them, then he would have to go under them. He dropped to his knees and slid through their legs, white lab coats whipping his face.

"Get him! Don't let him out of this cabin!" Linas roared at the exact time Joseph rolled out on the other side of the scientists.

Joseph swung his fists, his hands meeting nothing solid, only white coats and air. He felt like he was drowning, until there was a loud thump and the path round him cleared. Joseph crawled over to the door and dusted himself off.

All around him was chaos. The cabin looked like a fight scene from an action film. Sal had one of the scientists by the waist and was dragging him into the cell. Camera and sound duo, Agnès and Clio, were on Linas's shoulders. Agnès was pulling the ends of his hair while Clio covered his eyes.

"Get off me!" He jabbed the scalpel in the air, poking the other scientists who were trying to fight off the rest of Mum's crew.

"Ouch!" one scientist cried. "You got me."

"I can't see, can I!?" Linas staggered back towards the window. "Get them off me now!"

Bursting through the commotion came Funmi, skidding on her knees towards Joseph.

"Go and find Nellie!" Sal shouted, helping Mona throw another scientist into the cage. "We'll hold them off as long as we can."

Joseph didn't need telling twice. He grabbed Funmi's hand and pulled her out of the door and towards the next cabin. He pushed open the door, his eyes scanning every inch of the room. One wall was filled with computer screens and a radio system. A few of the robo-birds were on the floor, attached to a charging port.

"Mum?" he shouted. "Where are you?"

"This must be the security hub" – Funmi rushed over to the screens – "where the cameras on the robo-birds feed through. Your mum's got to be on one of these screens."

Different images popped up across the screens every few seconds. Joseph saw the lake. The forest canopy. He saw the glass lookout built into the volcano and a helicopter perched on top. Figures moved inside the lookout, but they were too small to clearly see. He muttered a silent wish that Flo, Isaac and Marianne were safe. They still hadn't made contact on the walkie-talkie.

"There she is!" Funmi pointed.

The next image only lasted a few seconds, but it was enough. Mum was slumped in a chair in a small room. The chair was next to an open hatch and her hands were tied together. The window behind the chair was the same style as the window in the cage cabin.

"Mum's in the next cabin!" Joseph was already halfway out of the door. There was no time for carefully considered plans or sneaky manoeuvres. He and Funmi simply sprinted across the grass to the third cabin. He charged at the door and it flung open. Shocked, Joseph stumbled over the threshold and clattered to the floor.

"Alright?" Funmi held out her hand.

"Fine." Joseph got to his feet. "Where is she?"

The cabin looked lived-in, with a small single bed pushed up against one wall and a table with an empty plate and glass. There was a toilet and sink on the other side and a pile of dirty clothes scrunched into a ball.

Funmi nodded towards a door at the back of the cabin and drew her finger to her lips. "Do you hear that?"

It was only once he'd calmed his breath that Joseph heard the sound too. It was barely a whisper coming from the other side of the door. It was the sound of a person doing their best to survive. He rushed forward, his hands shaking as he grabbed hold of the doorknob and stepped into the next room.

Time suspended as Mum slowly opened her eyes and shifted in the chair. Her long hair was matted, twisted in clumps, and her face was weary, flushed and marked with lines. But when she looked up at him, Joseph's world finally righted itself.

"Jojo Bean?" Mum croaked.

Chapter 34

THE SECOND LIFE OF PERCY PARISH

Flo's entire body tingled when she heard Uncle Percy's voice again. It was like communicating with a ghost. Finding Mum had always been the reason for the journey to Fantome Island, yet the voice she'd just heard in the lookout had taken Flo back to family parties when she was smaller and they'd play musical chairs. That rhythmic voice, which would always shout out "stop" and judge whether she or Joseph had sat down first, was one she thought she'd never hear again.

So Mum's scribbled theories in her hidden office were true. Uncle Percy was alive! Maybe everything would be okay. The thought was a buoy that Flo flung herself at.

"Uncle Percy!"

Percy walked towards them. He looked the same as when Flo had last seen him, the day before he'd left for his solo sailing trip. The trip that was meant to have killed him. He had the same piercing amber eyes and diamond-shaped dimple and a smile like a symphony. Where had he been this entire time?

"Flo." Percy's voice cracked as he came to a stop next to her net. His wide smile disappeared and he placed a hand over his heart, his dirty lab coat crinkling underneath his palm. "How glad I am to see you again. However, I wish it was under better circumstances. Frederick, please. The nets."

Flo's hope of a happy ending fractured when she saw how Uncle Percy looked at Frederick. He wasn't afraid. Percy wasn't a prisoner like they were. All would not be okay. She slowly righted her camera; whatever happened next needed to be recorded.

"The nets are necessary." Frederick wandered over to the sofa and slipped the remote control into his jacket pocket. "They broke into my office, took the coordinates, made their way across the ocean *and* found my island. I'm not taking any chances with these kids."

"What's going on?" Isaac looked between Flo and

Percy. "Aren't you on our side?"

"It's a complicated matter," Percy replied, a measure of kindness on his face. "I'd hoped that Nellie would've left the mystery around my disappearance alone, but she's always been as stubborn as a bull."

"Because she loved you." Flo choked. "We all loved you. You were family. When you died, we were heartbroken. Especially Jojo."

Percy brightened at the mention of her brother. "Is Joseph still a budding marine biologist?"

"You gave up the right to know anything about us when you disappeared!" Flo's breathing turned ragged with rage. "What happened to you? Why are you here?" She pointed at Frederick. "Are you working with *him*?"

Frederick's cheeks turned a violent red. "It's awfully rude to talk about someone like they're not in the room. You should be thanking me, really. When Percy told me of his idea, I was immediately on board. We sailed across every ocean looking for a place for him to carry out his work in secret until it was perfected."

"I'm sorry for faking the sailing accident and the pain it caused your family." Percy rubbed the side of his neck. "But I had to vanish to continue my life's work. My project required absolute privacy."

"The Weaver," Flo said, everything slotting into place as she looked at Percy and Frederick, two people that she thought she'd known rather well. "That machine is your creation, isn't it? But what's it for Unc—" She stopped herself; the word didn't feel right any more. Percy had lied too much. He was no longer family.

"I've always felt more comfortable in the natural world," Percy replied. "But the thing about the natural world is that it's inherently unnatural. I've never understood the human desire to categorize everything, to fit every living thing into a neat little box. So I explored the unnatural and discovered that there are no limits to what can be achieved."

"Stop talking in riddles!" Isaac shouted. "Get to the point."

Flo allowed herself a small smile, surprised and delighted at Isaac's refusal to cower.

Percy walked over to the bookcase wall and pulled a book from its place on the shelf. A screen unrolled itself from the ceiling, covering the bookcase.

"The Weaver is the ultimate tool for human adaptation," he said, pride seeping into every word. "As our planet warms and sea levels rise, life will become somewhat hostile for us humans. We have to find a way to survive – and my machine is the answer." Percy scratched his neck again. "After years of experimentation, I've found a way to merge the human body with the marvels of the natural world. Starting with the ocean."

Images filled the screen and Flo saw underwater cities populated by half-human, half-amphibian creatures. Fear and fascination gripped her. Percy had always been ambitious, but this was unlike anything she'd ever seen before.

"Think about it." Percy talked fast now, his hands conducting the air as he spoke. "What if humans had gills and could breathe underwater as well as on land? What if we could withstand severely high temperatures just like the Pompeii worm? What if we could live as long as the Greenland shark? The Weaver machine can expertly *weave* –" he chuckled "– multiple DNA strands inside a small black box. From this, new genetic codes are fed through to humans so that we can take on nature's best, adaptable qualities. It will help us *survive*."

"That thing in the lake that grabbed me," Isaac muttered. "It was one of your creations?"

Percy's eyes shone like marbles. "Ah, you met Bob, did you? Bob was the first of the scientists Frederick hired to work with me. He was a good sport, although the Weaver didn't quite get it right. Bob can only be on land for forty minutes before breathing gets tricky. He has to spend most of his time in the lake, poor chap. Our next test will require a tweak of the genetic code to get the balance right."

Flo felt like her lungs were filling with brine water. "So there's always a risk it might go wrong? You can't play with people's lives like that! Don't you remember anything Mum said?" She tried to reach the Percy she once knew, but he refused to meet her eye. "You don't mess with the ocean. You don't mess with nature. It doesn't belong to us."

"Nellie and I share different opinions about the natural world." Percy shrugged. "I'm so close to perfecting the technology, I can't stop now. Remember what I used to say about risks? Sometimes you just have to jump right in."

"But this is different!" Flo snapped back. "Even if you're doing this to help, you're still risking people's lives and the balance of the natural world."

"I have contacts all over the world who are interested in purchasing Percy's technology and none of them are worried about the *risk*." Frederick rolled his eyes. "The Weaver will be available to those who can afford it."

"Is this really what you want?" Flo's anger carried her on.

"I—" Percy started. "I want my technology to be available to everyone who needs it." He glanced at Frederick. "My work is for the greater good. For all of humankind."

"Laboratories don't come cheap, Percy," Frederick sneered. "If you want to carry on your research then you play by my rules. That was the deal you agreed to three years ago."

Flo waited for Percy to realize that he'd gone too far. She waited for him to remember the person he once was. She waited, but the moment never came. Whatever had happened in those missing years, she understood one thing. The Percy Parish she had once known was gone for ever. Another piece of her heart broke apart.

"Very well," Percy said, his voice smaller than before. "All I have is my work. Nothing and no one will stop me from achieving what I've always dreamed of. I'm blazing a trail for the future of this planet!"

"Good man, Percy. Too right you are." Frederick clapped his hands. "Our partnership will go down in history."

A creaking sound came from above and Flo looked

up at the metal hooks that held the nets. How much longer would they hold for? She was tired and felt the fight draining out of her. The plan for the Weaver was already in motion; how could she stop them and find Mum when she was trapped? How could she do anything?

"Please let us go," Flo pleaded. "Let us leave with Mum and her crew and we'll never bother you again. We won't tell anyone about what we saw here. We'll forget all about the Weaver."

"You know that's just not possible," Frederick replied. "It's not in a Wanderday's nature to give up so easily."

"Now you know I'm here, you'll never leave me alone." Percy took a step back, his hands rubbing the side of his neck. "I'm sorry."

Flo frowned. None of this was right. But there was something extra strange about Percy that she couldn't quite place her finger on. He was fidgety and on edge.

Frederick stood and walked towards the nets, the remote in his outstretched hand.

"Please," Flo begged. "Don't do this. Let us live."

Hesitation flickered in Percy's eyes, but it was quickly snuffed out. He retreated from the edge of the pool and walked back towards the doorway. He was leaving the lookout. He was leaving Flo again. It hurt even more than the first time.

Frederick stopped in front of Flo's net. He beckoned to her with his free hand. "Your pleas won't help you now. Don't think I haven't noticed what you're up to. Hand over the camera, Florence."

Flo instinctively tightened her hand over her camera. "I don't know what you mean."

"Don't play dumb with me, girl." Frederick laughed, a deep, hacking chortle. "I know you've been filming. You're not as sly as you think. Give it to me."

"Don't do it, Flo!" Isaac shouted. "Don't give away our evidence!"

Frederick smiled evenly and pressed the remote. Isaac's net jerked downwards, the bottom of it skimming the pool. The stonefish snapped their jaws at the surface.

"Stop it!" she screamed. "I'll give you the camera. Please, please don't hurt him."

Frederick walked to the pool's edge and tapped his feet impatiently. "Give it to me. Now."

"No!" Isaac shouted again, but Flo didn't listen. She twisted the camera through a gap in the net and stretched her arm as far as it would go. She'd find another way to expose Frederick and Percy. Nothing mattered more than getting off Fantome Island alive together.

"Throw it down, girl."

Flo could only watch as Frederick caught her camera and flicked through the recordings. Different emotions danced across his face and, as each minute passed, the chance of escape dwindled. Was this it? Was this how everything ended?

"Percy, do come and look at this," Frederick laughed. "Young Florence could have had quite the career as a film-maker."

"Can we get this over with?" Percy lingered by the doorway, looking down at the floor. "I need to get back for the next tests. Marianne de la Mer is already inside the Weaver. Once that's done, it'll be Nell—"

"No! Not Mum! Not Marianne!" Flo's cries could've shattered the glass lookout. She thrashed about in the net like a captive shark. "If there's a drop of goodness left in you, you'll leave them both alone."

A sharp cracking sound came from above. She looked up and saw a zigzag fissure working its way across the ceiling.

"What's happening?" Isaac asked.

The second crack was louder and the entire lookout shook. The nets swung from side to side and Flo gripped as tightly as her shaking hands would allow. “I don’t know,” she said.

“I do,” Percy said, his face reflecting the same fear as Flo’s. “It’s the volcano. It’s waking up.”

Chapter 35

BITTERSWEET REUNIONS

"Mum!" Joseph stumbled towards her in a daze. The cabin's back room was windowless and he narrowly missed the open trapdoor next to the chair she sat in. Are you okay?"

"I think I'm hallucinating. Is it really you, Jojo?"

"You're not hallucinating, I promise." Joseph reached out for her. "I'm here."

Funmi lit up the room with her watch-torch, illuminating Mum's tired, injured face.

"Oh, Mum." Up close her lips were cracked. Bruises, the purple of sunsets, had formed round a small cut on her neck. Joseph kept his expression steady and kissed her on the forehead. "What happened?"

Mum tried to sit up, but the rope dug into her wrists and she cried out in agony.

"Take it easy, Mrs Wanderday," Funmi said. "Slow, gentle movements. I'll cut you free."

"My little love. And Funmi too." Mum coughed and water spluttered from her mouth. She looked at Joseph with faraway eyes. "How did you get here?"

Joseph held Mum's hands steady as Funmi began to pick at the rope with her penknife. "I found your note and your secret office," he said. "Marianne found Flo and we've sort of been working together ever since. We couldn't just stay in Brinemouth. We came to bring you home."

"You came without Dad?" Mum's face wrinkled with worry. She looked over Joseph's shoulder to the door. "And where's your sister?"

"Dad would never have let us come here. We had to do this without him. And Flo. I—" Joseph faltered. "I don't know. She's with Isaac and Marianne. They went to find the lab, but they're not replying to our walkie-talkie messages."

"We need to find them!" Mum jerked forward as Funmi cut through the last knot. "If they're at the lab, they're in trouble." She gently touched her neck. "He tried to modify me, tried to give me gills."

Joseph felt furious and confused all at once. "Gills? Why?"

"I'll explain everything later, I promise." Mum shivered. "But right now we need to get to the laboratory." She slowly stood, Joseph's hand in hers as she found her balance.

"Frederick Titan will never hurt you again." He hugged her tight. "I promise."

"Oh, Jojo Bean," Mum whimpered. "It's not him. It's Percy."

"*Uncle* Percy?" Joseph's brain turned into scrambled mush. "He's alive? He's here?"

Mum shook her head. "He's not who we thought he was. He's been working with Frederick all this time."

In that moment, Joseph knew he'd never forget how he felt. He'd never forget how uncertain life could be and how people could be the complete opposite of what he thought they were.

And then the door behind them rattled in its frame.

Joseph braced himself for the worst as Mum pushed him and Funmi behind her. The worst being that Linas had escaped and was about to corner them in the cabin.

So, when the door opened and he saw the seven faces that made up Mum's crew, Joseph almost fell to his knees in relief.

"It's good to see you, Nellie." Mona, *The Ariel*'s doctor, grinned.

"You're all a sight for sore eyes," Mum replied. Her crew rushed over and bundled her in a great hug.

"What happened to Linas?" Joseph asked.

"We locked him and the others up." Sal laughed. "Got him to talk too. Seems Linas isn't so brave when threatened with his own scalpel. This trapdoor leads to the laboratory."

Joseph peered into the tunnel. It was a small drop to the dirt floor below.

"Come on." He jumped down without hesitation and the ground crunched underneath his feet. "We've got to find the others."

Mum, her crew and Funmi joined Joseph in the tunnel and they walked the long, uneven path. Funmi's watch-torch illuminated the way ahead and the tunnel walls, made from rock and dirt, seemed to hum.

"You're quite the leader these days." Mum looped her arm through Joseph's as the tunnel veered sharply.

"I'm a work-in-progress."

"Aren't we all," Mum murmured.

The air turned warmer the further they walked through the tunnel. Joseph felt the sweat dripping from each part of his body: the back of his neck, the crooks of his knees… He was uncomfortable, but he pushed on. The walls grew louder too. Their hums turned into shakes, rumblings that came and went like the tide, building each time.

"Is that normal?" Funmi asked, nervously.

Joseph looked to Mum and her crew for reassurance, but there was none to be found. They all exchanged worried glances. No one said the words *earthquake* or *eruption*, but they weren't far from everyone's thoughts.

"Let's get a move on," Mum said.

Ten minutes later, Joseph's knees felt like they were about to crack when the tunnel levelled out and opened up into a corridor. The floor and the ceiling turned from rock to metal. Here the air felt even hotter and he wiped his face with his hands.

"We're almost there!" He spotted a door at the end of the corridor and ran towards it. "Argh!" Joseph cried as he touched the handle.

"What's the matter?" Mum rushed to him, her energy and strength growing every minute.

"The door handle is so hot." Joseph waved his hand in the hope it would somehow cool. "It burned me."

"Hang on." Funmi grabbed her jumper from her rucksack. She wrapped it round her hand and pulled on the door handle. This time it swung open and they rushed into the adjoining room. As the door swung shut behind them, Joseph saw it was a bookcase on hinges.

"I remember this place," Mum said. "It's the lab, where Percy did this." She pointed to the cut on her neck.

Joseph swallowed down a sick feeling as he scanned the lab. He tried to focus on finding a way out, but his eyes lingered on the strange posters and specimens in jars. If Percy had tried to give Mum gills, was he trying to create the half-human, half-fish people that were on the posters in this room? The experiments were starting to piece together, but Joseph still didn't understand why. What was the point of them?

Joseph shook his head and looked around again. He had to concentrate on finding Flo. There was a door at one end and an open passageway at the other. There was a cabinet slightly covering the passageway, as though it had been moved recently.

"Help!" a voice screamed from the passageway. "Someone, help me!"

Joseph recognized the voice instantly and pointed. "That's Marianne! Her voice came from down there."

"Are Flo and Isaac with her?" Mum asked. "I can't hear them."

Joseph recalled the grainy figures he'd seen on the security screens. "I think they're in the lookout. I saw four people up there. Maybe they got separated from Marianne."

Mum made a choking noise. "If they're alone with Frederick and Percy we have to get to them now!"

A decision, Joseph knew, needed to be made and fast. He turned to Sal, his face set. "We have to split up. If you and the crew go and find Marianne, she can lead you back to the submarine." Another quake, louder this time, made the jars on the cabinets rattle. "Once you free her, you need to get as far away from this volcano as possible."

"Roger that," Sal replied. The rest of Mum's crew saluted simultaneously.

"We'll go to the lookout and find Flo and Isaac." Joseph thought of the steps carved into the volcano rock that led to the lookout and prayed that they would hold. The volcano, and the area around it, seemed to be growing increasingly unstable.

"But how will *you* get away?" Sal asked. "What if there's not enough time for you to get back to the sub?"

Joseph remembered something else he'd seen on the security camera screens. A golden helicopter sitting atop the lookout. An unlikely, but possible, plan began to form in his head. "I've got an idea," he said. "Trust me."

And with that the newly reunited friends and family broke apart once more, to carry out their own rescue missions.

Chapter 36

AN UNLIKELY SAVIOUR

Percy's words rang loud in Flo's ears. Time had suspended since he'd said the volcano was waking up. Now with every rumble and quake that made the lookout shake, Flo felt her chance of survival slipping away.

"We must protect the Weaver at all costs!" Frederick cried. He marched over to Percy and grabbed his shoulder. "Can you move the machine? Can you save it?"

"Not all of it." Percy squirmed under Frederick's grip. "It's too heavy."

"You must try!" Frederick urged. "Get down there now and salvage what you can. We haven't worked this hard for nothing."

"We?" Percy blinked.

"Just get on with it, man." Frederick pushed Percy towards the doorway. "I'll prepare the chopper. We need to get off this island before it blows."

"What about us?" Flo called.

"Yeah," Isaac shouted. "You can't just leave us here!"

"Oh we can." Frederick's head snapped back in their direction. He held Flo's camera in one hand and she cringed at his every move, imagining it smashing into a thousand pieces on the rocky floor. "You'll disappear along with this island. As for your pathetic attempt to expose me," he raised the camera above his head, "this is one documentary that will never see the light of day."

Flo closed her eyes, bracing for the inevitable sound of a thousand tiny camera shards. She dug her nails into her palms, trying not to think about everything she was about to lose. She waited and waited for the heart-breaking sound to come, but it never arrived. In its place came something else, something entirely unexpected: the thump of a body falling on the ground. She opened her eyes to a magnificent sight.

Joseph stood at the edge of the pool holding her camera like a trophy. Funmi was by his side with Frederick's remote control in her hand. She clicked a button and the stonefish pools disappeared underneath an iron grate. The nets slowly lowered down to the ground.

"You should be more careful with your camera, sis," Joseph smiled. "I hear there's award-winning footage on this thing."

"Let me go!" Frederick squirmed on the floor, trapped under the tentacle grip of Mum. Mum! Glorious, tired but triumphant Mum. Joseph had found her. And after everything she'd been through, she still had fight left. It doubled Flo's own strength.

"Mum?" Flo cried. "You're okay!"

"Of course. How could I not be? My hearts have come to take me home." Mum smiled. "Jojo Bean, pass me the rest of that rope, will you? I'm going to secure my old pal here."

"Nellie, please." Frederick's voice was angelic. "It doesn't have to be this way between us."

"Oh do shut up, Frederick." Mum's full energy was returning; her words crackled like sparklers. "You made it this way. We've got Flo's footage. When we get back to Brinemouth it's over." Mum tied the rope round his arms and legs. "There," she said, "that's better."

Funmi sliced through each net with her penknife, creating holes wide enough for Flo and Isaac to squeeze through. Joseph returned Flo's camera and she looped the strap round her neck. She no longer felt like an empty film roll. She was full again and she flung herself at Mum.

"Where's Percy?" Joseph asked.

"Didn't you see him on your way up here?" Isaac asked.

"No." Funmi glanced around. "We didn't pass anyone on the stairs. He must've left a different way."

Another quake, this one much longer, dislodged chunks of rock from the ceiling and Flo dodged a spear of rock just before it shattered on the floor.

"We need to get off this island, now," Mum said. "Forget about Percy."

"But we can't!" Flo protested. "We can't let him get away with the Weaver! He was going back down to the lab to save it. We need to destroy it. His experiments are too dangerous to continue. We have to stop him."

"Flo." Mum brushed her cheek with her hand. "We've got a recording of Frederick and Percy's confession. This volcano is going to blow soon. Percy won't be able to save the Weaver in time. It'll be destroyed, just like us if we don't leave now."

"But—" How could words accurately express all of the fury and betrayal Flo felt inside?

"Your mum's right." Isaac stood at the lookout window, his mouth open in shock. "It's already starting."

Flo rushed over to the window and looked out at the island. Lava flowed down the volcano, gathering speed as it headed towards the lake. It spat and fizzled and great plumes of grey smoke filled the sky. Malfunctioning robo-birds fell from the sky like rain.

As the lava reached the lake edge, she spotted a figure emerging from the water. She looked through her camera and zoomed right in. It was a man, covered head-to-toe in green-blue scales. Sharp fins ran in a straight line down his back and his hands and feet were webbed.

"That's Bob the scientist," Flo whispered. "Percy's first creation in the Weaver. He can't breathe out of water for long." She watched as he ran towards the cliff slope that led to the forest.

"I hope he makes it to the ocean in time," Isaac said.

"You two!" Joseph's voice pulled Flo away from the window. "We need to get out of here. We're taking the helicopter."

Mum pulled Frederick up by his shoulders. "Lead the way."

"You're taking me with you?" the old explorer asked, surprised.

"Did you think we'd leave you here to perish?" Mum patted Frederick on the back. "We wouldn't give you an easy escape like that. Oh no, you're coming back home with us to face the music. Now how do we get to the helicopter pad?"

"Very well," Frederick muttered. "Over there." He pointed to a painting that hung on a wall. "Turn it upside down."

Funmi, who was closest, did as instructed. She rotated the painting and, as it reached halfway, a panel in the wall opened to reveal another staircase. Mum frogmarched Frederick up the stairs first and the others followed. Flo saw the darkening sky above her; it wasn't yet early evening but the volcano had brought midnight to the island.

Frederick's helicopter was parked in the middle of the lookout roof. TT-01 was printed in golden letters on one side. The helicopter was huge, its blades sharp, and Flo wondered how such a machine could float in the sky. "Who can fly this thing?" she asked.

"I had flying lessons when I joined The Titans!" Mum sized up the helicopter. "At least one good thing came from working together, eh, Frederick?"

Frederick grunted in response.

“Let’s make this thing fly!” Joseph ran straight for the cockpit door. Flo realized, too late, that the door was slightly ajar. Like someone had recently got on board. She opened her mouth to warn her brother, but Joseph had already jumped straight into Percy’s grasping hands.

Chapter 37

GREAT ESCAPES AND ERUPTIONS

"Not so fast." Percy slithered down from the cockpit, holding Joseph against him like a shield. "This is my ride out of here."

"Uncle Percy. Please." Joseph wriggled, desperate to turn round and see him properly again. Joseph had never expected a reunion with his uncle, but this was beyond his wildest dreams. Because it wasn't a dream, but a nightmare.

"It's so good to see you, Jojo," Percy whispered. "My, how you've grown. I'm sorry it has to be this way."

Mum stepped forward. "If you hurt a single hair on my son's head, I promise it'll be the last thing you do. Let him go. It *doesn't* have to be this way."

"I'm afraid it does," Percy replied, a sob in his throat.

"Did you make it to the Weaver?" Frederick asked. Joseph noticed how his eyes grew big at the mention of the machine.

Flo's face twitched and Joseph looked at her. Her eyebrows jumped up and down and her eyes looked over his shoulder. Was she signalling to him? What did she want him to do?

Percy nodded solemnly. "I managed to save its key component – the black box that creates the new genetic codes. Everything else will perish in the lava, unfortunately. But I can rebuild the tank and the compartments."

"Excellent, excellent. The black box is all we need."

"No, Frederick." Percy cleared his throat. "There is no more 'we'. From now on I work alone. I'm leaving this place *alone.*"

"What?" Frederick spluttered. "You're leaving me here with them? After everything I've done for you? You ungrateful cretin!"

Mum pulled on the rope around Frederick's hands. "Keep quiet."

This time when Joseph locked eyes with Flo, he understood what she wanted him to do. As Percy and

Frederick argued, Percy's grip had grown loose enough for Joseph to slip away. Flo had been looking over his shoulder at the cockpit, where the keys were still in the ignition.

"I won't keep quiet!" Frederick shouted. "I am outraged! I created you both. Thanks to The Titans, the world knows your names. I *made* you. Percy, if you leave now without me I will destroy you. I promise."

"You'll have to find me first," Percy replied. He laughed and brought his hands to his mouth. As he did, Joseph seized the opportunity. With a slick step back, he jumped up into the cockpit and twisted the keys free from the ignition. There was something else on the passenger seat: the black box that Percy had mentioned. The essential part of the Weaver.

He scooped it up before jumping back down onto the lookout roof. He only had seconds to pull himself upright before Percy was stalking towards him, his teeth bared like fangs. Joseph saw his face and it frightened him. This wasn't the uncle he'd once known.

"Joseph!" Percy lunged towards him, but he rolled out of the way, nearing the roof edge. "Give the black box back. You're a man of science." His tone changed as he spoke, the anger turning to gentle reasoning. "You must understand why I need to continue and perfect my work. Hand back the keys."

The volcano roared as a new fissure opened and red-orange lava shot up from the ground. The rooftop shook and Joseph struggled to stay upright. He crawled over to the top of the staircase, dragged himself up and pulled back his arm. "If you want them, go and get them!" He released his grip and two objects whizzed through the air, landing with a thunk back inside the lookout.

Percy wailed. "What did you do?" He pushed past Joseph and scarpered back down the stairs.

"Jojo!" Flo ran towards him. "What *did* you do?"

"Relax." Joseph unfurled his left fist, revealing the keys in his palm. "I threw a couple of rocks. As for the black box, I just moved it under the seat. It's still inside the helicopter."

"You genius!" Mum grinned. "Right, everyone. Get in now!"

Joseph and Isaac jumped in first and climbed through to the back seats. Flo and Funmi joined them at the back, after helping Mum secure Frederick in the passenger seat.

"Nellie," Frederick wrung his hands. "Perhaps we

could come to some sort of arrangement once we're back in Brinemouth."

Mum pulled the cockpit door shut and fastened herself into the pilot's seat. "The only arrangement we'll be coming to is with the police once we hand you over. Now, please, Frederick, really do shut up." She stuffed a rag in his mouth before twisting the key in the ignition. "I need to concentrate."

The circuit board lit up and the blades began to whir, their forceful noise drowning out the sounds of the active volcano. The helicopter thrummed and lifted slowly from the ground.

Joseph fastened the seat belt across his lap. Flo and Funmi sat opposite him, their hands intertwined. Isaac closed his eyes and Joseph turned to the helicopter window, giving his best friend a moment while he muttered a prayer.

Through the window, Joseph saw Percy standing at the top of the staircase. His face was contorted in shades of fury and his white coat and trousers were torn. Joseph watched in horror as Percy ran across the roof, his arms outstretched. Time stretched thin as Percy flew through the air. He reached out with his arms and grabbed onto the landing gear, the metallic legs of the helicopter.

"Oh my god!" The others couldn't hear Joseph's cries over the sound of the blades. He frantically pointed at the window, mouthing *Percy*. Flo unclipped her belt and squashed next to Joseph, the siblings looking down at Percy dangling below.

Sweat poured down Percy's face and arms, seeping underneath his fingers. His grip was surely getting weaker and Joseph felt his heart tugging in opposite directions. No matter the lies and terrible things that Percy had done, he couldn't just sit here and watch him struggle. But what could he do?

Joseph reached for the door handle, but Flo pulled his hand back.

No, she mouthed.

So Joseph watched helplessly as Percy's fingers slipped one by one from the metal pole. He looked up, the veins in his face bulging under the strain of holding on. And then Percy gave up. It happened so quickly Joseph couldn't be sure of what he saw, but he swore then that his uncle had chosen to let go.

Percy fell through the air, growing smaller and smaller until he was swallowed by a huge moving cloud of gas and ash.

Flo rested her head on Joseph's shoulder, but he

didn't feel it. He was numb. He'd found and lost Uncle Percy all over again in the space of minutes.

As they rose higher above Fantome Island, the volcano erupted again. This time the eruption shook the sky as well as the land. Molten rock catapulted into the air around them and the helicopter swerved left and right, dodging the danger as it climbed higher in the sky.

Joseph reminded himself he was safe. They'd saved Mum and her crew, they'd found proof of Frederick's environmental crimes and captured his confession on camera. They even had the black box that powered the Weaver. He didn't fully understand the extent of Percy's experiments, but he was going to. He wanted to know the full reason his uncle had disappeared from his life.

Joseph took a deep breath as the helicopter flew over the ocean. He closed his eyes and thought of home.

Chapter 38

HAPPINESS THAT GLOWS IN THE DARK

Mr Pilcher had declared, in no uncertain terms, that the residents of the Fortunia were banned from talking to any of the journalists stalking the courtyard day in, day out. The head concierge had done his best to keep the media buzz to a low hum ever since the Wanderdays had returned home ten days ago, but even he couldn't stop the tidal wave of camera crews arriving, all hoping to land an exclusive with the family of the hour (and their friends).

Flo and Joseph had barely left Mum's side after returning from Fantome Island. They'd been there when she'd opened their apartment door and Dad had rushed towards them like they were all desert mirages.

They'd held her hands while she made an official statement to the police and had helped her and Marianne box up every piece of evidence they'd collected against Frederick Titan during their years of investigation. It included copies of all of Flo's recordings from their journey and time on the island. The Weaver's black box, however, had stayed underneath Joseph's bed. The Wanderday family felt that it was safest with them. Percy's technology would remain a secret for now.

Marianne was staying with the Wanderdays, turning their once tidy guest bedroom into a chaotic mess that almost rivalled Joseph's room. She and the rest of Mum's crew had made it back to the submarine in time, leaving Fantome Island behind as the lava swallowed the land.

Much to Joseph's relief, Dr Moray's research submarine had been returned to Brinemouth Port unscathed.

As for Frederick himself, he was to remain under police custody until he was brought to trial for the various crimes he'd been accused of. Loyal devotees had already gathered outside Brinemouth Prison to protest his innocence. Flo and Joseph had avoided that part of the city since getting home.

Life after Fantome Island had almost returned to

normal, except they hadn't seen Funmi or Isaac since returning home a week ago. The look on the faces of Maduka and Angela Aderemi and Sam Kessler, when Mum had landed the helicopter at Brinemouth Airport, had achieved more than any telling-off ever could. Guilt had consumed Flo and Joseph ever since, but they'd managed to sneak in a few forbidden phone calls.

"Baba has calmed down, but Mum's still on one," Funmi had told Flo. "She keeps saying that they didn't work so hard for me to throw it right back in their faces. I don't think I'm leaving this flat until the day of my funeral."

"Actually, Dad's been kind of nice." Isaac had sounded surprisingly cheerful, much to Joseph's delight when they spoke. "He's worked shorter days since I got back. We've had dinner together every night!"

Flo and Joseph had sought refuge in the cinema room more than usual since their return. It was a safe place, away from the madness unfolding around them. The journalists and photographers would soon grow bored and find another scandal to report but, until then, the brother and sister watched the news on a continuous loop, waiting for the update that they thought might never come.

And then it did.

The police had completed their search of Fantome Island – what was left of it – following the map coordinates that the Wanderdays had provided. The volcano had decimated the entire forest, leaving only charred tree skeletons in its wake. The pyroclastic flow, a fast-moving mix of hot lava, rocks, gas and ash, had buried the cabins and turned the lake into a mudflow.

Percy Parish, however, was nowhere to be found. International police teams had swept what remained of the island as best they could, but there was no trace of the scientist.

Watching the news, Joseph knew that Percy couldn't have survived the fall from the helicopter. It was impossible that he could be alive, wasn't it?

But Percy had already escaped death once.

Could he somehow do it again?

After fourteen long days the journalists finally shipped out and the four friends were reunited at last. Flo and Joseph spent the day at Plankton Park with Funmi and Isaac, enjoying a "supervised" picnic organized by Funmi's mum. It had been full of games, food and fun and afterwards, the adults had decided that Flo, Joseph, Funmi and Isaac could all hang out together again. They were just under one strict order: not to go anywhere near the ocean.

After hugging Mum and Dad goodnight, Flo crept down the hallway and knocked on her brother's door. She was too buzzed to sleep after spending the entire day in the park.

"Come in," a sleepy voice called.

Flo crept across her brother's surprisingly tidy bedroom floor and slipped under the duvet. "Fancy a sleepover?"

"Only if you don't fart."

Flo threw a cushion at Joseph's head. "Says you."

"Have you started working on your project yet?" Joseph asked. "The documentary?"

"Nope." Flo tossed and turned. "I haven't felt ready."

Ten minutes of silence passed. Both assumed the other one was asleep.

"Would you help me with it?" Flo broke the quiet between them.

"Really?" Joseph turned on his side and stared,

bright-eyed, at his sister. "You want to make the documentary together?"

Flo nodded. "If you want to. I couldn't have done any of it without you."

Joseph's smile might as well have been decorated with fairy lights; it lit up the dark room. "When do we start?"

"How about tomorrow?"

"It's a plan." Joseph nodded. "You know, I don't think I'll believe half the stuff on your camera. I still can't believe it all happened."

"I suppose that's what adventures are like. You're not always ready for what's about to happen."

"True. I don't think we were ready for any of it. We managed, though."

"We sure did." Flo rolled onto her side.

"I keep thinking about Uncle Percy."

Flo stiffened. "Don't call him that."

"But he was our uncle! I can't just forget about all the good times we had."

"I know," Flo replied. "I haven't either. But he did something unforgivable, Jojo. We can't forget about that either."

"He was trying to make the future a more hopeful place, wasn't he?" Joseph retorted. "I don't think he was such a bad person. What he was doing was different from all the things that Frederick did. The Weaver was Percy's way of attempting to solve our world's biggest problem."

Flo sighed and pulled the duvet higher round her neck. "I'm not sure. It's complicated. Humans shouldn't exploit nature for their own gain. We already have all the tools to save ourselves, to prevent a world where we need to live under water. It's not too late. We just need to wake up and use them."

"True." Joseph yawned, the word stretching in his mouth. "I just wish he'd talked to me, us, about it before. Maybe then he wouldn't have gone off with Frederick. Maybe he would've stayed."

"Don't beat yourself up with all the maybes." Flo moulded her head further into the pillow groove. "Anyway, we better get some sleep. We've got a lot of work to do tomorrow."

"Night, sis."

"Night, bro."

Flo closed her eyes and let the sounds of her city rock her like a lullaby. Brinemouth had always been her home, but there was something different about it now, something extra special and precious. She'd wanted adventure all her life, and she'd finally got it by the bucketful.

Yet, at that moment, there was no other place she'd rather be than on the tenth floor of the Fortunia.

Chapter 39

NOW SHOWING: JOURNEY TO FANTOME ISLAND

Eight months later…

"You're going to eat your own finger if you carry on like that."

Flo bit off a loose nail and narrowed her eyes at Joseph. "Says the boy who hasn't stopped clicking his fingers."

Joseph hopped down from the dressing-room table. "I'm not denying that I'm nervous. Because I am."

Flo exhaled and smoothed the creases of her star-patterned dress. "Alright, fine. I'm nervous. Actually scratch that. I'm terrified. Does that make you feel any better?"

He grinned. "A little bit."

Tonight, Brinemouth Amphitheatre buzzed like a hundred beehives. Every seat was sold out and the refreshment kiosks were running dangerously low on Cousteau's Confectionery and bottles of kelp cola. After all, it wasn't every day that a new Wanderday documentary premiered.

Especially when it wasn't a film by Nellie Wanderday, but her children instead.

There was a knock on the door and Joseph flinched. He was braver than he'd ever felt before, but the fear of what he'd seen on Fantome Island still lingered. He wasn't sure it would ever go away.

"Enter!" Flo swivelled in her chair to find Mum standing in the doorway. Her flowing hair was tied back in its usual ponytail and an orange anemone was tucked behind her left ear.

"I heard that there are two film-making prodigies in here." Mum smiled as brightly as her coral lipstick. "Could someone please direct me to them?"

Joseph laughed and ran to Mum for a hug.

Flo opted for a handshake instead. "I'm one of them. Flo Wanderday. Soon to be a famous documentary maker and co-creator of the most popular doc of all time."

Mum laughed. She pushed aside Flo's hand and pulled her in for a triple hug. "Of *all* time? That's fighting talk, my girl. I haven't retired just yet. In fact, I just received news of a very interesting project."

"You have?" Joseph looked up at her.

Flo tugged on Mum's sleeve. "What is it?"

"I'll tell you after the screening. Tonight isn't about me."

"But you're not going to—"

"Go off exploring without you both?" Mum finished Flo's question. "No. I don't think I could quite imagine doing that ever again. If there's anything I've learned, it's that I'm pretty useless without you two."

"We could've told you that." Joseph grinned.

"I better get back to my seat before your dad orders another extra-large bucket of popcorn." Mum kissed the tops of their heads. "Good luck, my little wandering wonders."

The stage lights shone brightly on Flo's and Joseph's faces. They could only see the people in the front row. Mum and Dad sat either side of Marianne, their parents chatting away with their honorary aunt. Isaac and

Funmi were both dressed in blue and were currently fighting over a fizzed-up bottle of kelp cola. Sal, Mona and the rest of *The Ariel*'s crew whispered among themselves. Thankfully, these were the only faces the brother and sister needed to see to calm their nerves.

The audience had just sat down again after standing to applaud their appearance onstage. Joseph hadn't shrunk back from the attention as he'd suspected he might. Flo was proud of her brother, even if he was squeezing her hand so tight it had started to feel numb.

"Thank you!" The microphone squeaked with feedback and Flo winced. So much for a smooth and confident start. "We're honoured that so many of you are here tonight to watch our film. As I'm sure you'll know, we created this film during the disappearance of our mother, Nellie Wanderday."

"It was a difficult time." Joseph stepped forward to share the mic. "But we always had belief. Hope was what kept us afloat during our journey to Fantome Island."

"Our mum always says that she'd follow a good story to the ends of the earth, and we're no different." Confidence flowed through Flo's voice now. The audience were hanging on her every word. "We could never have predicted how this story turned out and how we managed to unearth the truth about who Frederick Titan really is. But we couldn't have told this story without the help of our best friends. Funmi Aderemi and Isaac Kessler. And both an old and new friend: Marianne de la Mer."

Marianne whistled and stomped her feet.

"We also uncovered another story, one that we weren't expecting to find," Flo continued. It's a story about Percy Parish, our uncle, who we believed to be dead."

Joseph fiddled with his bow tie. "It's obvious that I'm not the most confident person in the world. But Mum always told me that there's strength in not always wanting to be seen. For every brave explorer there is a reluctant passenger, someone who doesn't realize their true potential. This film is for both of those people."

"You're about to watch the world premiere of *The Wanderdays: Journey to Fantome Island*." Flo bowed. "We hope you enjoy it."

The audience clapped as Flo and Joseph took their seats next to their best friends.

"Smashed it," Isaac whispered to Joseph. "Couldn't even tell if you were peeing your pants."

Funmi squeezed Flo's hand. "Iconic behaviour.

Thanks for my shout-out. Does that make me famous now too?"

"I think so. Just don't let it go to your head."

A hush fell over the audience as the curtains parted and the screen rolled down. Flo and Joseph settled into their chairs, ready to experience the most extraordinary adventure of their lives all over again.

ROLL CREDITS

Look out for

THE WANDERDAYS

next thrilling adventure where Flo, Joseph and their friends must journey into the Frondoso Forest to uncover its secrets – ancient and new!

#TheWanderdays
@ClareFPovey
@Usborne

Clare Povey is an author, avid language learner and the proud owner of four Blue Peter badges.

She wanted to be a marine biologist when she was younger but found science difficult and so decided to create stories about the wonders of the natural world instead.

Her first novel for younger readers *The Unexpected Tale of Bastien Bonlivre* was a Waterstones Children's Book of the Month and was inspired by her time studying French at university and living in Lille.

She has dealt with Obsessive Compulsive Disorder (OCD) her entire life and now writes stories about characters who have adventures and are forever curious about the world, despite their intrusive thoughts.

Acknowledgements

Thank you to my agent Kirsty McLachlan, for the constant support.

This book made it into the hands of readers thanks to the brilliant team at Usborne. I couldn't be more grateful for their belief in my stories and I am incredibly proud to be published by them.

The biggest thank you to Ben Mantle for his gorgeous cover illustration.

Thank you to Melissa Cristina Márquez for her expert ocean knowledge, Max Goldbart for his advice on Isaac's character, and Ayo Okojie for sharing her experiences and considerations that helped shaped Funmi.

Thank you to my friends and family who helped me through the highs and lows while I worked on The Wanderdays.

As ever, thank you to Adam for everything and for being by my side for every season of life.

My parents, for their love and unwavering support. My mum, who first helped me understand my OCD and her daily reminders that I am more than the sum of all my thoughts.

Joseph Wanderday is a character I've wanted to write for a long time. Like me, he has OCD and this manifests mainly as distressing, intrusive thoughts. Over the course of the story, he learns more about himself than he ever thought was possible. I don't have it all figured out in my own life, so I didn't want Joseph to suddenly be in control of his brain at the end of the story. That doesn't ring true for me. What I wanted to show was that children, and adults alike, with OCD and intrusive thoughts can still go on adventures. You can be heroes and live life your own way.

Finally, a thank you, dear reader, for joining me on this adventure.

Clare Povey

Clare Povey is also the author of the BASTIEN BONLIVRE adventures.

Classic stories about friendship, hope, bravery and the power of imagination.

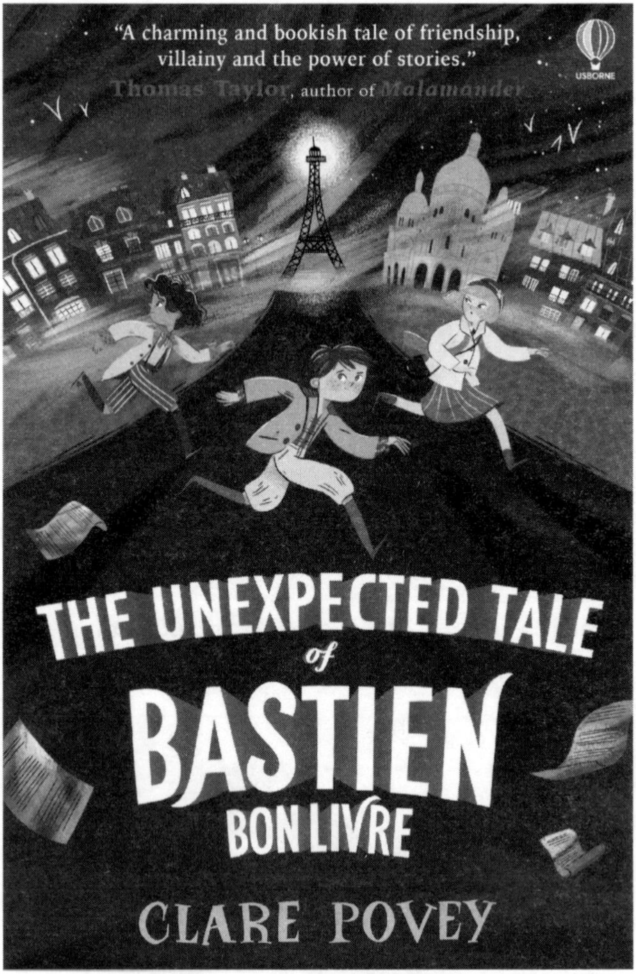

BASTIEN BONLIVRE is a boy with a big imagination, determined to finish the story his parents started, left to him in a red notebook.

Olivier Odieux and his villainous brothers are masterminding their greatest plot yet...

What connects these two stories is a dangerous secret, a hidden mystery and an unexpected race across Paris for the truth. Can Bastien and his friends Alice, Theo and Sami be brave enough to stop Olivier stealing the ending they deserve?

"A *charming bookish tale of friendship, villainy and the power of stories.*"
Thomas Taylor

A BASTIEN BON LIVRE ADVENTURE!
USBORNE
THE UNEXPECTED TALE
of the
BAD BROTHERS
CLARE POVEY